Praise for *Making Peace with Suicide*

"Suicide is one of our most painful, difficult, confusing and wounding of human experiences. Dr. Adele McDowell addresses this topic with love and beauty. She non-judgmentally restores empathy, compassion and understanding. She courageously offers deep tending in a "place of primal pain." And she is comprehensive, sharing the history, complexity, universality, and even positive dimensions of this mysterious act. Whether you are contemplating or have survived the attempt, lost someone to suicide, or counsel and help these populations, Adele McDowell's *Making Peace with Suicide* will bring you hope, healing, compassion and understanding."

–Edward Tick, PhD
Director, *Soldier's Heart*; Author, *War* and *the Soul and Warrior's Return*

"With sensitivity and compassion, *Making Peace with Suicide* explores the depth and breadth of suicide and offers insights and healing. This book is essential reading."
–C. Norman Shealy, MD, PhD

"No topic could be more timely than suicide. This remarkable book addresses people who have contemplated ending their lives as well as those who have to deal with the aftermath of those who succeeded. But it will also be invaluable to mental health workers and military chaplains, especially those who deal with young people who have been bullied and veterans with PTSD. For such a complex topic, Dr. McDowell's writing style is reader-friendly and the stories she presents may well evoke tears. Her wise recommendations include teaching self-mastery techniques to help people cope with the stress of a success-oriented society. I have read many books on this sensitive topic, but none with the breadth and scope of *Making Peace with Suicide*."

–Stanley Krippner, PhD
Co-author, *Personal Mythology: The Psychology of Your Evolving Self*
and *Haunted by Combat: Understanding PTSD in War Veterans*

"Finally. A book that explains—in the simplest of terms, in a non-sensational, non-academic manner—the phenomenal, worldwide epidemic we call suicide. If you read one book on mental illness and how it affects our world, READ THIS ONE!"

–Ginny Sparrow, Editor, American Association of Suicidology

"Adele bravely and compassionately tackles a topic that many people avoid discussing—suicide. Yet in the understanding of it, the confusion and sense of loss is greatly eased. *Making Peace with Suicide* is rich with insight and healing methods all intended to help heal the void we feel when we lose a loved one to suicide. It's also written for those who are suicidal to help them understand their pain and despair, and to let them know there is always help and there is always hope. I wish I had this book to read when my best friend took her life."

–Carol Ritberger PhD, author of *Healing Happens with Your Help:*
Understanding the Hidden Meaning behind Illness

"This powerful book, written by a psychologist and former suicide-hotline responder, speaks to us all, about a present epidemic, surrounded by shame, taboo and secrets. Offering many personal stories, Adele helps the reader to find peace speaking to both those who believe they're the only person who has ever felt this desperate and to the survivors whose lives are thrown into turmoil. This excellent book, full of useful resources, is essential for everybody who feels alone with their issues of life or death, bringing greater understanding, acceptance and comfort.

–Christine Page, MD, seminar leader &
author of *The Healing Power of the Sacred Woman*

"As a minister/therapist for more than thirty years as well as a wife who lost her military husband to suicide, I have never found a more compassionate, effective book on suicide and its aftermath. This book serves many needs and highlights the myriad ways in which suicide changes one's life direction. I cannot say strongly enough how powerful and helpful this book is."

–Rev. Colleen E. Brown, Unity minister

"The loss of a loved one by any means is traumatic. When the loss is by suicide, in addition to the grief of the loss itself, survivors are often left riddled with guilt, anger, shame, and endless questioning, by both themselves and by others. In *Making Peace with Suicide*, Dr. McDowell gently and brilliantly weaves vital suicide survivor education with comforting and inspirational thoughts and quotes, all designed to direct the reader on a path of healing, resolution and peace. A must-read for anyone who has been touched by the tragedy of suicide and left to answer the question, 'Why?' "

— Carole Brody Fleet, award-winning and bestselling author of
Widows Wear Stilettos…; *Happily Even After…*; and
When Bad Things Happen to Good Women…

"A subject such as this is never easy to digest. However, with Adele's wisdom and guidance through her experience, this is a must read. We are in a new world now. Let Adele's wisdom guide you with her insights for a new perspective on suicide."

–Mona Delfino, author of *The Sacred Language of the Human Body*

Making Peace with Suicide

A Book of Hope, Understanding, and Comfort

Adele Ryan McDowell, PhD

McDowell, Adele Ryan, PhD

Making Peace with Suicide: A Book of Hope, Understanding, and Comfort

"A Psychologist's Suicide," "How do You Make Sense of a Sudden Death?" and "Grief: Yours, Mine, and Ours" were originally published on UPI's *Religion and Spirituality*, *The Examiner*, and *Self Growth* online sites.

"Call Back Your Spirit or Die" was originally published on UPI's Religion and Spirituality and Shaman Portal online sites.

© "A Star" by Gabriel Rosenstock

The poem "Imponderables" by Dianna Vagianos Armentrout was originally published in *The Vermont Literary Review Summer/Fall 2009, Volume XI, Number 1*. Used with permission.

Cover design by Meredith Blevins. "Summer Tree Illustration" by *Adyna@istockphotos.com*

Author photograph by Cynthia McIntyre.

Library of Congress Control Number: 2014918896

ISBN: 978-0-9821176-2-0

1. Suicide—psychology. 2. Suicide survivors—self-help. 3. Understanding suicide—psychology. 4. The nature of suicide—spirituality.

This book is dedicated to my mother, a lost and broken soul,
who struggled through life fighting her demons and, in the process, became one
of my greatest teachers.

You taught me well, Mother, and I am most grateful.
Hope this finds you splashing about in the light,
knowing what a great job you did.

Contents

Introduction

*If we have no peace,
it is because we have forgotten
that we belong to each other.*
— Mother Teresa

*I*deally, peace is our natural state. More often, peace is hard-won. It takes lots of practice to find peace and lots of hard work to create, much less maintain, a state of peacefulness. When peace does come, it can be a blessing or a miracle. We can take a full breath. We are no longer conflicted or distressed. We have learned to let go, allow, and, most importantly, accept, even the unacceptable.

With peace, we reclaim the vital energy needed to support our life and future happiness. Peace is the root of all healing. Without peace, there is no healing, and we hemorrhage our own life force.

For survivors living in the wake of a loved one's suicide, it is my desire and intention for this book to provide a deeper understanding of suicide, expand your compassion about this difficult topic, and bring you some comfort and peace.

Included in this book are stories from survivors, an overview of the many influences that can lead someone to suicide, thoughts for your consideration, a healing methodology to help you make peace, an enhanced perspective, and resources to promote healing.

For readers who are suicidal, my hopes are these: You will find understanding and compassion for your pain and despair. You will feel encouraged when you read the shared wisdom of those who have been on the brink—like yourself. You will realize that life can change, that it rarely stays static. Your place in the world is important to us.

My goal in writing this book is simple: I want to take judgment off the table as a response to suicide. It is time for a heightened state of compassion for those who have chosen suicide, for those who have been left behind holding their hearts and dreams in their hands, and for those who are considering suicide as an option.

It is time for healing and peace to begin.

Deep Peace, Deep Peace

Deep peace, deep peace of the running wave to you;
Deep peace of the flowing air to you;
Deep peace of the quiet earth to you;
Deep peace of the shining stars to you;
Deep peace of the gentle night to you;
Moon and stars pour their healing light on you.
Deep peace to you.
Deep peuce to you.

—Traditional Gaelic Blessing

Chapter One

Context: Why this book?

What Does Making *Peace* with Suicide Mean?

Make peace.
Find peace.
Rest in Peace.
Be at peace.
Give peace a chance.
Peace be with you.

eace is part of our everyday language. The word is familiar. It conveys warmth. It speaks of an absence of war, conflict, and struggle. Peace rests in the geographic center of grace. Its voice is calm, tranquil, and serene.

When we are peaceful, we are no longer at odds with the world, our loved ones, or ourselves. We are not being defensive, nor are we playing the offense. We are detached and neutral. We rest in emotional and mental balance. Free-floating, we are nurtured in a sweet pool of equilibrium.

Peace is a word that is rarely associated with suicide.

When I spoke with some colleagues and friends early on in my writing process, they were concerned that this book, *Making Peace with Suicide*, might mean a reader must agree, condone, or even support a loved one's suicide. Of course, that level of acceptance is very unusual.

The suicide of a friend or family member spins those who are left behind in a dervish dance of disbelief, grief, and, sometimes, anger. We hold fast to the idea that we are wired to live, to fight for life, and even to thrive. When a suicide happens, the world—and our perception of it—turns upside down.

When you are very sick and the prognosis is poor, you look to your doctor and other practitioners for all possible treatments in order to recover your health and well-being. If held at gunpoint, you would probably pray for your life. Suicide is the antithesis of that urge to survive; it is often defined as an act of violence against the self. However, for some, suicide may seem to be the one act that will bring release from suffering.

Yet, there is nothing peaceful about the aftermath of a suicide. It is confusing, infuriating, heartbreaking, and guilt-inducing.

From my perspective, making peace with suicide means you have found a way to understand, forgive, reconcile, and accept. This acceptance of "what is, is" allows you to find peace with the sudden, shocking death of your loved one at a time when you are feeling anything but peaceful.

How Do We Talk about Suicide?

When I began this project several years ago, my colleagues and friends often glanced at me, puzzled, wondering why I would want to dive into such a dark topic. Now, given the widespread number of suicides across the world and the fact that we are finally beginning a real dialogue about this taboo subject, they understand.

As a psychologist and former hotline responder, I have had a good deal of experience dealing with people on the brink of suicide. I understand the pain—physical, emotional, mental, psychic, or any combination thereof—that causes a person to believe that suicide could be the best, sometimes the only, solution. I understand the anger and rage of survivors who are bewildered and feel they are left to clean up the mess, literally and metaphorically. I understand the guilt and regret that can hold a survivor's heart hostage.

Suicide is messy. It is weighted with shame and secrecy, criticism and judgment. Too often there is little compassion for those who have chosen to end their lives. Compassion or support for the survivors of suicide is often embarrassed and spare. Surviving loved ones are traumatized as they hold the remains of a shattered life in their hands. They are full of questions, recriminations, and their own mixed emotions. *Why did this happen? Why didn't I see this coming? What did I miss? Could I have done something more?*

In some conscious or unconscious way, outsiders tend, ultimately, to hold the surviving loved ones responsible. Survivors not only question themselves, they may also blame the systems within their respective cultures—schools, mental health care, military, government, corporations—that failed to notice, help, or protect their loved one. The shadow of a suicidal death expresses a failure that leaves unanswered questions and complicated grief in its wake.

There is no right and wrong here. Each life is a river with its own course, and the pain results from a confluence of different factors. There is not one cause; there is no one answer.

Impacting every level of society and every corner of the world, suicide is a tangled web. From a clinical perspective, it is fascinating, sparking endless debate, methodologies, and opinions. However, when suicide hits close to home, it is no longer a subject of detached inquiry and research. It is shocking and bewildering. It is a sucker punch to the gut. It is a gaping hole in the heart.

Over the past few years, I have spoken with survivors who have lost people they loved and have generously shared their remarkable journeys. I have debated with practitioners, interviewed people who have attempted suicide multiple times, and have read the personal stories of survival following a suicide. I have scanned Google alerts and read papers from educational, psychological, and psychiatric associations. Searching out all possible resources and curious about expanded perspectives, I have also questioned teachers of higher consciousness and mediums.

I certainly don't have all of the answers. Quite frankly, I don't think there is one answer—suicide is a complex topic. And, it is happening across the globe with greater and alarming frequency.

In this book, we will:

◈ Open the door and air out the subject of suicide as a whole. It is not endemic to one particular group or defined place. It is an epidemic that is raging across our globe.

◈ Explore suicide from various perspectives to enhance our understanding and compassion.

◆ Offer comfort, hope, and shared wisdom to the survivors who have lost loved ones through suicide, and help free these survivors from the enormous weight of grief and heartache, shame and blame.

◆ Offer understanding, compassion, and perspective to those who are in a place of deep pain and considering suicide as an option.

◆ Provide an expanded view of suicide that may open a door to a more peaceful resolution and reconciliation.

◆ Encourage acceptance, compassion, non-judgment, and conversation.

We will explore the depth and breadth of suicide. Think about the six-degrees-of-separation concept. We all know someone, or, at the very least, we know someone who knows someone, who died by suicide or attempted suicide. Suicide is universal.

The number of suicidal deaths has ratcheted upward exponentially with global wars, bullying, addiction, and economic crises in combination with too-fast, disconnected, joyless lifestyles. We can't sweep this topic under the carpet anymore.

Harsh reactions are beginning to soften and change with this shocking upsurge. They are also changing because we are beginning to talk about suicide, but we still have a very long way to go. Sharing our experiences is important. Healing doesn't happen in a murky basement. It happens under the light.

At the end of this book, you will find a resource section. It is not encyclopedic and all-inclusive. It is meant to be a jumping-off point for your own investigation.

My biggest hope is that you can find peace around the unsettled loss of your loved one, and that you can find peace within yourself during the times you walk an unsteady and painful path.

My Story

My first brushes with suicidal behavior were accidental. My mother was a depressive and a serious alcoholic who was never professionally diagnosed.

Around the age of twelve, I noticed that both of my mother's wrists were covered in huge scabs and scars. I knew immediately she had tried to kill herself. My parents were going through a fractious, bitter, and seemingly never-ending divorce. My mother allowed that the doctor had injured her. That made no sense to me. No doctor would carve up a person's wrists. My mother continued to deny her suicide attempt, as she did many other things, but I knew, without a doubt, that was her intention.

Maybe a year later, one Saturday morning, I woke up very early, climbed out of bed and got completely dressed, shoes and all. I was dressed as if I was going out, but I had no plans. This was strange behavior in our household; my mother encouraged my sister and me to roll over and go back to sleep on Saturdays. She wanted us out of the way so she could drink and dial—meaning, she'd call her friends and tell stories, frequently embellished or fictitious, about her family.

My mother was shocked to see me up and about so early. She spent the next three hours trying to convince me to go back to bed. I refused to budge. There was nothing she could say or do. It was an unspoken standoff and we sat for hours, staring at each other. I knew that I could not leave my mother alone. I had to keep her safe. At some point in the late morning, the energies shifted and I relinquished my guard duty. My mother was, for the moment, safe again.

In my first year of college, I stayed up all night, sitting at the bedside of an older student. I held the razor blade she had just used to slice her wrists. It was stained with her dried blood. I would not let go of it, and I would not leave her. To this day, I cannot recall how I ended up doing that for a woman I didn't really know, but maybe that was the point.

During the night, I was her faithful watchdog, and the next morning she was doubled over in shame and embarrassment. She was ashamed, not only because of what she had done, but because there were many others in the dorm who knew what had happened. By way of an apology, she bought us a communal box of candy and made each of us promise never to speak to her—or anyone else—about the incident. She later transferred to another school.

Working the hotline

In my senior year of college, during the early 1970s, I volunteered, with a handful of female students, to be part of the first paraprofessional suicide hotline in the country. I remember little of the training, but I do remember one part of the application form that was replicated during our interview with the psychiatrist. He wanted to know about our monthly cycles. Specifically, he wanted to know the exact number of pads that we used on a daily basis during our monthly periods.

There was no accounting for tampons, so I made up an answer that I thought sounded normal. Apparently, I'd hit upon the right number. I was approved to begin volunteering on the hotline.

Over the years, I have wondered about the psychiatrist's focus on our menstrual flows. Why was this information so critical to our work as suicide hotline responders?

This takes me to a story by Harvard-trained biologist and mind-body-spirit expert, Joan Borysenko, PhD.

Following a prescient dream, Joan visited her doctor, concerned about a mass in her breast. The doctor told Joan that she was hysterical and she should do something about her stress. Joan laughed—she had written a best-selling book about stress. Joan sought out a second opinion, and surgery was recommended. The surgeon excised a mass that was about to turn cancerous. Joan was relieved and overjoyed that she had trusted her instincts and listened to her dream.

Joan was bothered that her first doctor told her she was hysterical, and that led her to some interesting research. She found that the word "hysteria" comes from the Greek, and it means "wandering womb." This was a hilarious revelation. Imagine this: a legion of wandering wombs, a.k.a. hysterical women, walking around the world. Clearly, there would be unbridled chaos.

Perhaps that's exactly what concerned the psychiatrist. If his female volunteers were menstruating, they could be on the verge of hysteria and wandering dispositions. That would certainly not bode well for his new hotline.

The hotline work itself was carried out in long shifts, like those of medical students, at a phone station next door to the hospital's massive spaghetti-style switchboard. (Remember, this was the early 1970s.) The switchboard operator was a salt-of-the-earth, crusty, no-nonsense, and terrifically funny woman with bleached, blond hair and an infectious laugh. As it turned out, she was my comrade-in-arms when I received those crisis calls.

Many of the hotline volunteers got bored with the job. They worked long hours and rarely received a call. The opposite was true for me. I did receive calls, few by today's standards, but it was big-doings then.

All my calls were from men. They were ready to jump from the top floor of a parking structure, shoot themselves and others, or ingest a massive quantity of alcohol and pills. I talked with them and, mostly, I listened. If I was lucky, I made a connection with my caller and, maybe, he came to trust me a little. If the call was serious, and most were, the switchboard operator traced the call and notified the police. The police raced to the scene that I had carefully, and cautiously, extracted from my caller. (This was long before the days of GPS and caller ID.) Most of these men called from pay phones and, frequently, multiple pay phones to avoid any kind of trace. They were loath to give me their locations for fear of the police showing up and carting them to the hospital. Of course, that is exactly what happened.

The psychiatrist had assured us, his hotline volunteers, that we would never meet our callers. They were to be transported to a large community hospital and given a physical and psychological evaluation. We did not expect them to arrive at the smaller, strictly psychiatric, hospital where we were based.

However, each and every one of my callers, with their police escorts, ended up in the lobby of our psychiatric hospital. Each man asked to speak with me. I was terrified to meet them, unprepared, and awkward. I was afraid they would be angry with me for sending the police and violating their trust. Some were, but others weren't.

I always felt, and still do, that when someone calls for help, it's because a part of them wants to be rescued. It's the part that yearns for a potential solution or a window of hope and possibility. We all share a very human need for connection. We all want to feel we matter to someone. And, the idea that someone really cares is critically important for those still considering the pros and cons of suicide.

In my psychotherapy practice I have talked clients off ledges, out of their cars, and away from ropes, belts, razor blades, knives, firearms, heroin, and pills.

I have reminded them of who they are in better moments and the differences they have made in the lives of their loved ones. I have asked if this is the legacy they want to leave their family and the memory they want their children to carry. I have reminded them that they are not alone in their pain, and that we can walk through this together.

My responses have varied as I've tried to meet my clients in that direct, raw, primal place of pain. I have been gentle; I have been tough. I have argued points and positions—we can all get stuck in the ruts and mazes we have created for ourselves. I have made suicide contracts[1] with people on the edge.

---

[1] A suicide contract is an agreement by the client to make direct (telephone or in-person) contact with his/her therapist before any dire action is taken. This inserts a pause and allows for connection, conversation, and, hopefully, a reframe of the situation.

Sometimes, I have talked karma and the afterlife. Other times, I have insisted on hospitalizations and discussed medications.

The priority, of course, is safety. And safety can be a huge variable. Moods and humors can shift and twist and turn. Some moments are better than others. The middle of the night is rarely good. Circular thinking, irrational reasoning, paranoia, reruns of heartbreak and failure, screaming demons, incessant internal chatter, the battering ram of self-judgment, and the weight of self-hate are frequent nocturnal visitors for the psychologically fragile. These emotional and mental gyrations are debilitating and destructive. They can be a ramp toward disaster.

And like everyone who does this work, we listen for the subtle shift in tone, the muffled word, the point of fury. Whatever it is, we want to understand the heart of their pain and see what we can do to alleviate the suffering, create a place of hope, and maintain personal safety.

A Psychologist's Suicide

Because of the loss of a colleague and friend through suicide, I began exploring what it means to lose someone in this way. (That exploration became the primary inspiration for this book.)

When I was first told that Susan had died, I wasn't given the full picture. There was a lot of hedging until it all finally spilled out—it might have been …well, it actually was … a suicide. There were questions and concerns. There was no communication from her family; they had firmly closed and locked that door. Each of her friends and colleagues held a tiny piece of the puzzle. We put our heads together, trying to make sense of this incredulous news.

In working my way through thoughts and feelings, I wrote the following essay. It helped me make peace with Susan's sudden departure.

The word came last week that a friend and colleague, a clinical psychologist, had committed suicide. She had suffered a hammering of profound losses and fell into a deep hole of depression. She had placed herself in good professional hands, was hospitalized for two weeks, and then released with medications and a discharge summary that she, herself, could have written. She later took her life by overdose.

If you are a clinical type, then you might be interested in knowing that she, we will call her Susan, had been hospitalized once before as a young adult due to a breakdown of sorts. That initial breakdown shaped her career. I believe that it enhanced Susan's humanity and made her more accepting of the mysteries of life. Susan was a very skilled and gifted therapist. Over the course of her professional life, she had helped so many find their way to safety and sanity, which makes it even more incongruent that this healing-type woman would take her own life.

Susan was a huge dreamer—big, significant dreams, healing dreams, dreams that reverberated in her 3D life with books, pictures, and images tumbling, on occasion, from her walls and book shelves. Susan analyzed dreams with her patients; she explored their multi-nuanced aspects with her colleagues. Susan understood the imaginal world and the power of metaphor to transform a life.

Yet, with all those gifts and talents, Susan's well of despair flooded. Taken hostage by her biochemical influences, she crossed the borders of her inner terrain and entered the place without light, with nary a crack in the darkness. All her training and education notwithstanding, suicide seemed the answer to Susan's distraught and off-balanced self.

Suicide is not painless; it leaves loved ones—and in her case, patients, too— reeling in disbelief and "what if's" and "If only, I had. . . ." We think, perhaps, we could have done something differently, made a move or said the right words that might have tipped the balance in favor of life. Death is not easy on a regular basis, but it becomes tainted and shame-faced when described as a suicide. It's as if we, the survivors, have failed to do our part. We feel responsible. And, sometimes, we are angry, too. "How could they?" we puzzle, as if it really had anything to do with us.

As a psychologist, as well as a former suicide hot-line responder, I understand all too well what might lead up to those moments when suicide is considered. Within that tight, airless thought-process, suicide can become an option to end the torment.

I get it. I'm not saying I like it, condone it, or anything else, but I understand how someone can get there. I understand the trajectory of suffering. I have witnessed the desperation of unabated pain—be it physical, psychological, or both—and the dark places that pain can take someone. I have seen how a life can crumble in on itself, worn down by the struggle, the relentless struggle.

That much pain changes a person; it leaves an indelible mark. Suicide becomes all about moving out of the desperate pain. It is a very intimate act. It is self on self, in all of its swirling eddies of emotional tumult. There is little room for anyone else.

There are many paths of pain and despair. Suicide may be an impulsive act of fury and pain. For some, it is a release from the daily torment that makes life unbearable. For others, it is a door out of the suffocating room where they cannot draw a deep breath, much less consider compassion for the self. Suicide is an act of violence against the much-hated, broken, and wounded self.

The act leaves a wake of questions. I have opted to forgo the questions. It does not change anything. What I know is that my friend was in pain, was biochemically unbalanced, and made a choice. I wish her choice had been different, but who am I to say? Her death teaches me about the fragility and the ferocity of the human spirit.

In the aftermath, I have come up with what I think is the perfect antidote. I am sending loads and loads of light to my friend, Susan. It seems like the perfect thing to do after so much darkness. And, who knows, maybe it will help her soul find its sparkle again.

When I reread this piece from 2011, I realize that my thinking and language have evolved and unfolded since then. For example, now I avoid using the term "committed suicide." More importantly, I know there is nothing simple about suicide and there are times when suicide is not an act of violence. On the contrary, it may be an act of peace.

Again, suicide is a very complicated topic.

*L*ove is never late.

— Maye Shaw

Chapter Two

Understanding suicide

Why Understanding Is Helpful

After you have lost a loved one to suicide, you feel anything but powerful or strong. Most likely, you are at your most vulnerable, full of heartbreak and deep grief.

Suicide leaves a trail of questions and uncertainties. Knowledge can help make some sense of the unimaginable. When we learn more, we have a basis for comparison. We realize, perhaps, that our situation is not so unusual. Plus, we can accept more fully the biochemical or psychosocial elements that have led to a suicidal action. When we understand more, we are no longer so confused, confounded, or upset. We find steadier footing, and we find ourselves more emotionally and mentally stable. Indeed, knowledge can serve as a powerful healing ally.

This chapter, "Understanding Suicide," examines suicide with a neutral and objective eye. It is filled with facts, figures, and my observations from 30+ years in the consultation room. You will find a historical perspective, the primary factors, snapshots of suicide, and the three common elements that can influence suicidality.

This chapter will, hopefully, help you understand the phenomenon of suicide within a larger context and, in doing so, offer you some solace and, perhaps, some answers to your concerns.

A Very Brief Historical Perspective

Suicide has been part of the human experience, across the globe, as long as we have been recording our history. Over the centuries, suicide has been perceived as a personal choice, a mortal sin, a social issue, a mental illness, as well as an act of honor, piety, or shame.

In ancient Egypt, it is said, "There is no direct archaeological evidence for suicide . . . nor for any discriminatory treatment of people who died at their own hand."[1] In other words, suicide did not break any laws or codes. There was no taboo against it.

Romans and Greeks (with the exception of Pythagoras for mathematical reasons, and Aristotle due to his belief in a finite number of souls and the consequences of same) were not troubled about suicide.[2] Roman and Japanese soldiers were known to take their own lives if defeated in battle. It was considered a point of honor or a 'patriotic suicide' and may have also served as a way to avoid capture and possible torture.[3]

Early Christians, often en masse, chose voluntary death and martyrdom in lieu of persecution. These suicides were considered a great act of piety.[4] In the fourth century, St. Augustine was the first Christian to publicly declare suicide a sin.[5]

During the Middle Ages, a time that was deeply influenced by the venal actions of the Roman Catholic Church, suicide was shrouded in great shame and fear of eternal repercussions. If you took your own life, your body became an object of public ridicule and torture. You were excommunicated from the Church, your property was seized, and you were prohibited from burial in consecrated or sacred ground.[6]

Suicide moved out the Dark Ages and became a topic of social interest during the Renaissance and Reformation. Shakespeare, as we know, wrote of suicide in a

---

[1] www.reshafim.org.il/.

[2] Wikipedia.com, The History of Suicide, http://en.wikipedia.org/wiki/History_of_suicide.

[3] Wikipedia, The History of Suicide, http://en.wikipedia.org/wiki/History_of_suicide/.

[4] Arthur Drodge and James Tabor, *A Noble Death: Suicide and Martyrdom among Christians and Jews in Antiquity* (HarperSanFrancisco, 1992).

[5] www.crouchfoundation.org/.

[6] Wikipedia.com, The History of Suicide, http://en.wikipedia.org/wiki/History_of_suicide/.

number of his plays,[7] as did the poet John Donne.[8] The philosophers Voltaire and Montesquieu also defended an individual's right to choose death.[9]

As detailed in the appendix, French sociologist, social psychologist, and philosopher Émile Durkheim wrote *Le Suicide* (1897). This book was the first social analysis of suicide, and it helped increase awareness of suicide as well as decrease the shame.

Sigmund Freud stepped onto the world stage in the early twentieth century, and with his arrival, mental illness was first viewed as a medical condition. Studies in psychiatry and psychology blossomed; suicide awareness, education, and treatment strategies were created. In 1983, the Roman Catholic Church reversed its canon, and those who died by suicide could have a Catholic funeral and burial.

Today, suicide is a worldwide epidemic that is indifferent to the boundaries between cultures, age, religion, gender, and socioeconomic classes. Suicide has many faces, and each one is part of humanity regardless of our differences. Suicide may be a response to despair, pain, illness, and the pull of inner demons. It can be an act of war, a reaction to violence, or a final surrender.

The Primary Factors Leading to Suicide

We know that today suicide is a worldwide epidemic. We understand that methods may differ, but are there certain root causes that lead to suicide?

Statistical research tells us that 90% of all suicides are due to one of these three causes:

1. Mental illness

2. Substance abuse

3. Mental illness *and* substance abuse

From a clinical point of view, we're quite familiar with these categories, and perhaps we even take solace in them. These are patterns and trends that make sense. They indicate that the person was not in his or her right mind and acted out of skewed thinking and emotions.

---

7 Anthony and Cleopatra, Hamlet, Julius Caesar, Othello, Romeo and Juliet.
8 "Bianthanatos," Donne's poem in defense of suicide.
9 www.crouchfoundation.org/.

Both mental illness and substance abuse batter the psyche, and they can kick the stuffing out of an individual, leaving the person emotionally tattered, with precious little strength to withstand the vagaries of life.

Psychotropic medications, meant to calm mental illness, can have major side effects and need to be monitored often. Both mental illness and substance abuse can turn a person from Dr. Jekyll to Mr. Hyde with little warning.

Further, mental illness and substance abuse are profoundly influenced by genetic factors and family histories that include substance abuse, mental illness, and suicides or thoughts of suicide.

There are many permutations to those three primary factors (see the appendix for specific risk factors and stressors). Suicide is not simple; it involves the body, mind, and soul.

Worldwide Snapshots of Suicide

The factors that contribute to suicide tend to play out in the real world, in real lives, in a multiplicity of ways that are highly individualized. Following are some real examples, primarily gleaned from my conversations and correspondence with individuals across the globe and supplemented with some stories reported in the national press.

◆ Across the country, almost once every hour, twenty-two times each day, a veteran takes his or her life.

◆ In New Canaan, CT, the phrase "died suddenly" is the euphemism for suicide.

◆ From Albuquerque, NM, a doctor writes, "Suicide is offensive. Get a life."

◆ In California, a teenager slashes his wrists because the voices in his head told him he was the last person alive on the planet, and he needed to kill himself to join the others.

◆ In Canada, a mother is questioned about why she is having her son's funeral in her local church since her son died by suicide.

◆ In Turkey, a teenage girl shoots herself in the stomach to avoid a forced marriage to her cousin.

◆ Two weeks before graduation, a college student hangs himself after his girlfriend does not answer his texts.

◆ In West Virginia, a survivor's group consciously chooses not to use the words "committed suicide." They find it insensitive.

◆ In France, a school-age boy plays a computer game with his younger brother. The boy loses to his younger sibling and goes into his bedroom and hangs himself.

◆ In Massachusetts, a teen comes home from school and finds his father hanging in the basement; on that day, he says, he became a man.

◆ In Spain, foreclosure agents repeatedly ring a doorbell; there is no response. They pound on the door; there is no response. The locksmith accompanying the team unlocks the door. There they see the 53-year-old mother standing on a chair on the sixth-floor balcony of her apartment. Upon seeing the agents enter her now-foreclosed home, the woman jumps off her balcony.

◆ A man travels to New York City to take his life. His note reads that he chose New York City because he could be anonymous there.

◆ A mom, dad, and younger son walk into their house. The mom sees it first, blocks her younger son's view, and sends him outside, as she and her husband rush to the body of their older son. He would no longer be bullied at school.

◆ In India, a farmer is repeatedly beset by a band of threatening debt collectors after his crop failed. Their terrorizing pressure is more than he can handle.

◆ A woman calls her adult kids and tells them all to come and visit on one particular weekend. She is very ill and wants to tell them goodbye, face-to-face, and ensure there will be no recriminations after she has taken her life.

◆ Just after his eighteenth birthday, during the Viet Nam War era, a young man in Detroit takes his life when he receives his draft notice.

◆ A mother in Texas stops taking her medication for postpartum depression. At the end of a day, she tells her husband she is running to the market for bananas. It is too late when her husband notices that there are bananas on the kitchen counter.

◆ In England, a husband trusts his intuition and leaves his job midday to hurry home. His wife is locked in the bathroom. He kicks the door open and finds his wife bleeding in the bathtub from razor cuts. This is not the first time. He gets his wife cleaned up before the kids come home from school.

◆ Even after a family moves a long distance away, a mother says her son was never the same following sexual abuse by a relative. He got into drugs and alcohol; nothing made him happy.

Suicide takes more forms than we can imagine. People in distress will seek a way out, a way that may seem incomprehensible to those left behind. Perhaps, though, surviving family and friends may find some relief, some comfort, in knowing that a loved one's death was not an anomaly.

To the world
you might just be one person,
but to one person
you are the world.

— No Attribution[10]

---

[10] There is no one source listed for this quote. It clearly resonates with many people, as it has been attributed to Anonymous, Boone Family Association of Cal-Mont in Montana, G.K. Chesterton, Victor Hugo, Paulette Mitchell, Brandi Snyder, Dr. Seuss, Bill Wilson, British soldier's WW II headstone in Normandy, France, and Unknown. It is also part of a children's story.

The Spectrum of Suicide

Like almost everything we experience, suicidality exists on a spectrum. Each of the following points carries a degree of severity. (Obviously some are more intense and critical than others, but each calls for professional help.) These points provide an approximation based on my professional experience. This is I how I see suicide portrayed in the consultation room:

Ideation

Quite simply, you are thinking about suicide. You are rolling the idea around in your brain. *Does this make sense for me? Would it be my answer?*

Gestures

This is a seeming attempt at suicide by self-injury without serious or fatal consequences. Cutting is a good example. (Let's be clear: this is not cutting as self-harm where the intention is to relieve crushing emotions or to be able to feel something.)

Suicidal gestures are a cry for help and, sometimes, attention. They are an alarm bell that requires professional help. These gestures are often labeled with the unfortunate term "para-suicide," which, to me, minimizes the gravity of the situation. Repeated gestures are frequently a precursor to a completed suicide.

Passively Suicidal

This is a form of suicidal ideation. You are thinking about it, but know at this moment you would never do it. It sounds like a plausible idea because you are in so much emotional pain. There is a level of resignation in this thinking. For example, if someone magically took you out of your misery, you would not fight back. You simply don't want to feel so much pain any more—you are so tired and depleted and paralyzed. You feel powerless to change the situation.

Active Thinking

This is a form of suicidal ideation that is farther along the spectrum. You are developing a plan. You are working out the details. You know exactly what, when, and how you will do it. For some, there is relief in having a plan. For others, there is a grim satisfaction in imagining the impact their death will have on others: *Maybe now they will understand how much I hurt.*

Thinking and Doing

There are two forms of thinking-and-doing; one is planned and the other is impulsive.

Planned: With the planned, you are now making a concrete plan. You are making preparations, securing necessary accoutrements, and orchestrating how you will make your suicide happen. Frequently, when individuals have reached this step, they may present themselves as happy to their loved ones and therapists. They have a plan of action. They are resolved and there is no more equivocation.

Sometimes, the plan is enough in and of itself and serves as a fallback position if everything goes horribly wrong. Further, when there are doubts, the plan can crumble and the individual may be open to outside intervention and assistance.

Impulsive: Impulsive thinking-and-doing is, as the name states, impulsive. It's a flash of a thought and a rush of feeling that makes sense at the time. It's a quick way to end the internal torment. This impulsivity can be accelerated by substance abuse that lowers the inhibitions, a history of risky behavior, unfettered anger, and unrelenting anxiety.

Chronically Suicidal

The chronically suicidal are individuals who, by virtue of mental illness, are always in and out of suicidality. Usually, they have been on psych meds for years and they have been hospitalized frequently. It is their default wiring and where they land when their pain escalates; their thinking contracts or becomes chaotic; and they want to escape from the effects of their medications.

Slow Suicide?

Is there such a thing? This is a subjective category. To some, yes, there is slow suicide. They have witnessed the full-blown anorexia nervosa, heroin abuse, and chronic alcoholism of their loved one. Slow suicide suggests a lifetime of self-harm and abuse that erodes a person's health, well-being, mental stability, emotional resilience, and vital energy. Slow suicide further suggests enormous unresolved pain (physical and/or emotional), grief, and anger on the part of the individual.

Suicide's Three Common Elements

From my perspective, all suicidal gestures and actions, no matter how large or small, injurious or lethal, share these three elements:

1. Pain

2. Disconnection

3. Disenfranchisement

Pain

Pain means any and all pain in all its permutations—be it physical, emotional, mental, spiritual, or any combination thereof. Pain hurts. When we are in pain, we have one goal: to stop hurting. We do everything we can to get out of pain. Often, we don't care what it takes to be pain-free; we just want the howling, can't-take-a-deep-breath or think-clearly pain to be over as soon as possible.

Constant, chronic pain—of any variety—changes people. Pain is exhausting and debilitating. Pain makes us cranky and intolerant. Pain wreaks havoc with our sleep cycle. It rearranges our thinking as well as diminishes our ability to cope and withstand the vagaries of everyday life.

When we are in pain, we contract into ourselves. Our world becomes smaller, darker, and enclosed. We shut out the world. There is only so much bandwidth, and we use it to manage the pain. The only thing that matters is to be pain-free, now. And, unfortunately, that can sometimes result in a suicidal action.

Disconnection

Disconnection speaks to the separation between the self and others. Separation is the operative word. We feel unwanted and unloved, alone and isolated, misunderstood and alien. There may be no one in our corner or no sense of connection with another person, a group of people, or a higher power. We can even feel profoundly disconnected among family and friends, who do not understand us and, more pointedly, do not comprehend what we have experienced and what has happened to us. This can be the height of loneliness.

We know from research that people who feel socially isolated (i.e., divorced, widowed, etc.) are at increased risk for suicide as compared with those who have responsibility for family members and are part of some kind of social grouping, network, or organization.[11]

With disconnection, it feels as if there is no tether to stay anchored and grounded on the earth plane. We are alone. No one gets us. This is particularly true of survivors of a suicide loss, the military and veterans, and survivors of childhood sexual abuse.

Disenfranchisement

Disenfranchisement, in the psychological sense, is disconnection to the nth degree. It is the ultimate sense of disconnection; it's as if we are looking at the world with our nose pressed to the glass. We do not feel that we belong, nor are we connected in any larger sense. We are no longer a part of the whole. We are a free-floating entity adrift in the world, alone, without value, purpose, or plan. There is no meaning in our life. We feel invisible and worth nothing. This is the utmost of pain.

We humans are wired to be connected. We are social beings, and relationships of any and all kinds are the bedrock of our existence. When we feel disenfranchised, we have lost our personal power and have become more vulnerable and defenseless. We feel ineffective and incapable. Disenfranchisement is a kind of existential pain that wears away our sense of self. Energetically, we begin to fade and disappear.

All three elements—pain, disconnection, and disenfranchisement—take us to shut-down, closed-off places. This leads to inactivity, inertia, passivity, and powerlessness. We feel stuck. We have lost our abilities to be creative and expansive. There is precious little energy or flow. And, from that position, it is easy to become dispirited and hopeless, which is another kind of pain. And pain of all kinds can lead to suicidal thinking and action.

---

[11] Deborah L. Trout, The Role of Social Isolation in Suicide, *Suicide and Life-Threatening Behavior* 10, no. 1 (1980):10–23, available online: DOI: 10.1111/j.1943-278X.1980.tb00693.

Suicide is a complicated and multi-factored issue, and yet there are three common elements that serve as the foundation to suicidality. These elements address the full spectrum of suicide. They can help us understand the ineffable "why" of suicide and, also, serve as warning flags for the future.

These three elements also underscore our need to find better ways to reach out and provide safety nets, support, and aid for our most vulnerable and traumatized.

The motto should not be:
forgive one another;
rather, understand one another.

— Emma Goldman

Chapter Three

What leads to suicide?

Suicide is the result of a confluence of factors, circumstances, pain, biological vulnerabilities, trauma, and more. In this chapter, we will take a more in-depth look at the causes of suicide to gain a better understanding of why the choice of suicide was made. This can help us make sense of the seemingly senseless and incomprehensible.

Out of fear, judgment, or lack of information, suicide has been misattributed to cowardice, weakness, and selfishness. *How could they do that to their family? They didn't have the guts to face their problems.* This chapter will shed some light on what leads to suicide. It is my hope that beyond those unconscious comments, there is a common ground where we are able to meet one another with understanding and compassion, knowing full well that most hearts beat alike.

Mental Illness

Suicide is considered a mental health issue. Why would someone want to take their own life? They must be crazy.

And, sometimes, they are. There are people who cannot function on a day-to-day basis, do not bathe for a year, receive messages to kill themselves or others, or believe their fillings are wired to Martian intelligence. There are very real neurological[1] and biochemical influences[2] that place these patients at high risk.

---

[1] Serious neurological issues like cluster headaches and trigeminal neuralgia, aka the "suicide diseases," also place patients as high risk.

[2] For some individuals, prescription medications (not mental illness) can create these adverse biochemical reactions. Certain medications even come with warnings about the potential side

Untreated depression is considered the number one cause of suicide.3 If you, or someone you love, has experienced the reality of major depression, you know what a devastating, debilitating, and a biochemical illness it is. The depressed person does not see or think clearly. She is locked inside a black, airless box that offers no light or perspective.

Hospitalization and medication have saved many lives. William Styron, in his memoir, *Darkness Visible: A Memoir of Madness* (1992), eloquently detailed his descent into, and recovery from, depression, which he called, "a howling tempest in the brain . . . dreadful, pouncing seizures of anxiety." Styron understood the stranglehold of depression: "The pain of severe depression is quite unimaginable to those who have not suffered it, and it kills in many instances because its anguish can no longer be borne."

Along with major depressive disorder, the psychiatric illnesses that can lead to suicidal actions are bipolar disorder (formerly known as manic depression), borderline personality disorder, post-traumatic stress disorder (PTSD), schizophrenia, and other psychotic disorders.

Did you know that the single greatest risk factor for suicide is a history of suicidal behaviors and attempts?4 Of course, this makes perfect sense, and if someone you love has these behavior patterns, take them seriously.

If you have lived with a loved one who has suffered from any of these mental illnesses, your life has not been an easy one. Nor has theirs. No one chooses to live with a debilitating psychiatric or psychological disorder that frequently moves in and out of crisis. It is painful, chaotic, exhausting, and terrifying for both the patient and loved ones. Ongoing treatment and meds are usually necessary to help make life more manageable.

A psychiatrist, a colleague of mine, once shared this with me: The majority of her patients who ended up in the hospital emergency room had stopped taking their medications, which then precipitated the subsequent disintegration.

---

effect of increased feelings of suicidality. This is not uncommon. For example, I was told of one gentleman who was on 12 different medications for his heart and related issues. The combination of drugs seriously altered him in a biochemical way; he became suicidal and took his life.

3 Suicide Causes, http://www.suicide.org/suicide-causes.html.

4 Suicide, National Alliance on Mental Illness, http://www.nami.org/ Template.cfm?Section=By_Illness&Template=/ContentManagement/ContentDisplay.cfm&ContentID=23041.

Nancy Kehoe, PhD, RSCJ, a Harvard Medical School professor, clinical psychologist, and nun, offered a new take on psychiatric hospitalizations during a lecture I attended decades ago in Boston. She allowed that for many of her patients, a psychiatric hospital gave them a much-needed sense of community and connection. And, with that sense of community and connection, they were able to heal. And by *heal*, I mean to find some stability so that they could return to the world as a functioning participant.

This made me think of the African tribes as well as many of the Indigenous people who work as a community and address the soul[5] to help those in pain (of any kind) to find relief. There are many paths to wellness and wholeness.

You Can't Shake Your Family Tree

In psychology, the continuing and great debate concerns nature vs. nurture.

Nature includes our DNA, genetic influences, and inherited traits, such as green eyes, curly hair, body type, and risk for certain diseases. In other words, it's the whole of what we carry forward within our physical, cellular selves from birth. Nurture refers to environmental influences, such as our family culture, upbringing, and education. In other words, nature is the seed and nurture is the garden.

Nurture starts the minute we are born, and we could well argue that it begins *in utero*. A primary example of nurture is your home environment. Did you grow up in a commune, with several generations of family members, on a farm, in a housing project, in a neighborhood where all the kids played together outside, an orphanage, a boarding school, or with a single parent? Were you bullied, beaten, abused, ignored, criticized, encouraged, spoiled, burdened, treated like the baby, or expected to be a grown-up? All your early experiences are important. They help shape and form you. Further, the family is our first social unit. This is where we learn to be, where we learn how people are treated, and what is acceptable behavior as defined by our family. It is also where we first learn to define ourselves through people's reactions to us.

Psychology asks, "*Does nature or nurture provide the greatest influence on an individual?*" The answer is that both are equally essential. That is why family histories are significant from both a medical and a mental health standpoint.

---

5 See Chapter 10 for more discussion of suicide and the soul.

It's important to know if you came from a long line of depressed, addicted, abusive, or violent people. Is there a history of serious mental illness in your family? Has anyone ended his life by suicide? It is not unusual to see a thread of suicides in a family tree—the taboo has been broken and it has become an acceptable option. Is there a gun in the home? Research indicates that a gun in the home increases the risk of suicide.[6] These patterns, both genetic and behavioral, influence your physical and psychological make-up and can place you at higher risk for suicide.

Pain

Pain does not discriminate. It moves among us equally, wearing many faces, including that of physical, emotional, mental, and spiritual pain.

Pain can look like a physical wound, broken parts, a speeding mind cycling through multi-dimensional layers, heartbreak, trauma, abandonment, shattered dreams, a wailing debate with God, homelessness, hunger, failed attempts, low-slung despair, high-pitched anxiety, self-hate, the endless push and pull of addiction, torture, and the intractable agony of chronic pain, among other conditions. Both cluster headaches and trigeminal neuralgia are called the "suicide diseases." The excruciating levels of pain associated with each disorder make the individuals want to die to be free of the inordinate pain.

Unrelenting pain can wear a person down. It feels as if it will never end. It feels like there is no solution. It hurts so, so much. That sort of pain can leave you breathless. And, that kind of fetal-positioned, tear-producing pain can prompt thoughts of suicide.

Cumulative Stressors, Crisis, and Trauma

A darling Celtic client of mine had a great saying, "Life does life." She was right. It does.

There are times when life throws us a major curveball and we are seriously rattled. We lose our footing, and our wherewithal is seriously diminished. If there are continuous stressors such as disasters, losses, medical conditions, and financial issues, a person who has been functioning well may begin to feel the onslaught, for it is akin to non-stop blows to the body.

---

[6] Firearm Access is a Risk Factor for Suicide Harvard School of Public Health, http://www.hsph.harvard.edu/means-matter/means-matter/risk/.

Stress is cumulative, and non-stop stress allows no room to take a breath, to process, or assess. You are going from one thing to another. Before you know it, you are holding on by a thread. Life has become overwhelming. There seems to be no meaning and no point to it all. You are psychologically shattered. Then one more stressor knocks at your door, and you can't imagine how you are going to keep going on like this. You have tried your best, but you are tired. You are worn out.

Think of the rash of "suicides by economic crises" in several European countries. Imagine the suddenly homeless, the ostracized and shunned, the failed crops, the medical emergencies, the bereft husband, and the bankrupt. They have endured much, and this accumulation of stress and being powerless can prompt suicidal feelings.

Be it an injury to the body, mind, soul, or an emotional shock that upends a life, trauma is pervasive in our world. Trauma can be a sudden death, combat service, childhood sexual abuse, a natural disaster, terrorism, catastrophic illness, and violence such as unrelenting bullying.

For some, that acute stress and shock of the experience(s) does not fade away or diminish; it becomes entrenched in an insidious way. The body-whacking, heart thumping, mind-numbing, horrifying, excruciating, and unfathomable traumatic experience holds a person hostage in a complete mind-body-heart hell.

This chronic pattern of neurological and physical responses is called post-traumatic stress disorder (PTSD). This is particularly prevalent, and most understandable, among survivors of childhood sexual abuse, victims of bullying, and combat soldiers. They are at high risk for suicide given the horrors they have lived through, have been tormented by, and have survived.

Imagine the VA Hospital and a group of vets waiting to attend a PTSD treatment group. Their hands are shoved into their pockets. Very few are holding cups of coffee because their hands shake from the increased cortisol in their systems.

Imagine the student who has been bullied to such an extreme that he cannot focus on his classes. He sits in terror waiting for the next attack and wondering how he can protect himself.

Imagine a sexual abuse support group. The women share their difficulties sleeping due to nightmares replaying nightly. The terror and the body memories flood their systems frequently; sleep is anathema. Pain is a constant companion.

For those in the hell of PTSD, suicide can be seen as an option to end the recurring cycles of pain and horror. Sometimes, too much is just too much.

Substance Abuse
and Addiction

◆ Drugs and alcohol increase the risk of death by suicide more than six times.[7]

◆ The largest risk factors for suicidal thoughts are depression and other mental disorders, and substance abuse.[8]

◆ More than one in three people who die from suicide are intoxicated, most commonly with alcohol or opiates (i.e., heroin, oxycodone).[9]

Addiction is a brain disorder, not merely a matter of willpower. The brain is held hostage by drugs and alcohol. It is a real disease that is both cunning and baffling. And, it is treatable.

The abuse of substances, drugs and/or alcohol, leads to ignoring your responsibilities, taking risks, relationship problems, and potential legal issues. You are using substances without concern for their impact. It's a bit like you have begun an unhealthy love affair. You are not quite yourself; you don't care what others say, and you become more and more entranced with your new "love." Slowly, and most certainly, you hand your power over to the substances of your choice.

Full-blown addiction harms the body, makes changes in the brain, results in poor life choices, and batters relationships. Addiction also increases feelings of self-hate, shame, isolation, and scheming behaviors. It erodes the spirit. Your life totally revolves around making connections, getting the substance of your choice, using that substance, and recovering from its use. Yet, you continue to use the drugs and/or alcohol even though you know it is bad for you. You are powerless, and the substances now own you.

Why do suicide, substance abuse, and addiction frequently go hand-in-hand?

---

7 Rebecca A. Clay, Substance Abuse & Suicide: White Paper Explores Connection, *SAMHSA News*, Vol. 17, No. 1 (Jan./Feb. 2009), http://www.samhsa.gov/samhsanewsletter/Volume_17_Number_1/SubstanceAbuseAndSuicide.aspx.

8 Substance Abuse May be Risk Factor for Suicidal Thoughts or Attempts, from *Addiction Treatment Magazine*, citing the National Institute of Mental Health, posted October 1, 2010, http://www.addictiontreatmentmagazine.com/addiction-news/substance-abuse-may-be-risk-factor-for-suicidal-thoughts-or-attempts/.

9 National Alliance on Mental Illness, Suicide, http://www.nami.org/Template.cfm?Section=By_Illness&Template=/ContentManagement/ContentDisplay.cfm&ContentID=23041.

We know that substance abuse changes us physically, emotionally, and mentally in these ways:

- Decreases inhibitions and lowers defenses

- Increases aggressiveness and violent behavior

- Impairs judgment

- Increases impulsivity. (Adolescents and young adults, especially, feel "bulletproof," and that nothing bad could ever happen to them.)

- Amplifies emotional responses such as hopelessness, despair, shame, and abandonment

- Increases and exacerbates emotional fragility already present within certain populations, i.e., those who are dual diagnosed (mental illness + substance abuse) and those suffering with PTSD and traumatic brain injury (TBI)

We know that substance abuse changes the brain. It impacts thoughts, feelings, and actions. Frequently, substance abuse is an anesthetic, a maladaptive habit-pattern, a coping response for stress, pain, and unhappiness. For the emotionally vulnerable person, substance abuse is akin to a match near a can of gasoline. There is a much greater potential for disaster.

Brain Damage

As we have discussed, the brain is doubly impacted by trauma and addiction. We also know that organic brain disease may increase suicidality, and there are worrisome side effects that come with certain psych meds.

Soldiers, football players, boxers, other high-impact sports athletes, car accident victims, and others who have had a traumatic brain injury (TBI) or its milder form, post-concussion syndrome (PCS), are at risk. TBI has two causes:

1. Penetration of the head by a foreign object, such as a gunshot or sharp object.

2. Strong jostling within the cranium from a fall, a blow to the head, a car or motorcycle accident, etc.[10]

---

[10] Centers for Disease Control and Prevention, http://www.cdc.gov/TraumaticBrainInjury/.

The hallmarks of TBI, depending upon the severity of the blow to the head, can be:

◆ Cognitive impairment, evidenced in poor memory and lack of focus

◆ Emotional problems, such as depression, anxiety, personality change, aggression, and impulse control

◆ Impaired motor function, poor balance and coordination, and weakness in the extremities

◆ Problems with vision, hearing, and touch as well as impaired perception[11]

NFL player Dave Duerson,[12] former star of the Chicago Bears, shot himself in the chest at age 50. Before taking his life with a self-inflicted gunshot wound to the chest, he texted his family, asking that his brain be given to Boston University School of Medicine to be used for research—which is why he shot himself in the chest rather than in the head.

Researchers in neurology discovered that Duerson suffered from a neurodegenerative disease called CTE (chronic traumatic encephalopathy), which is linked to repeated head trauma and promotes the growth of a protein that is prevalent in degenerating brains like those with Alzheimer's disease. The symptoms of CTE include suicidality, depression, aggression, and impaired judgment. [13]

In 2006, another NFL player, Andre Waters of the Philadelphia Eagles, ended his life at the age of 44.[14] The forensic pathologist who studied Waters's brain said that it resembled the brain of an 85-year-old man in the first stages of Alzheimer's.

The current research indicates that CTE is also found among military veterans and young school athletes, including those who play hockey and football, who take repeated blows to head.[15] The soft-tissue damage to the brain is cumulative and dangerous.

The brain damage caused by CTE and TBI can lead to suicide.

---

[11] Centers for Disease Control and Prevention, http://www.cdc.gov/TraumaticBrainInjury/.

[12] Alan Schwarz, Duerson's Brain Trauma Diagnosed, *NYTimes.com*, May 2, 2011, http://www.nytimes.com/2011/05/03/sports/football/03duerson.html?_r=0/.

[13] What is CTE? Boston University, CTE Center, http://www.bu.edu/cte/about/what-is-cte/.

[14] "Former Eagles DB Andre Waters, 44, commits suicide," *ESPN.com* news services, 11/21/2006, http://sports.espn.go.com/nfl/news/story?id=2669517.

[15] Frequently Asked Questions, Boston University, CTE Center, http://www.bu.edu/cte/about/frequently-asked-questions/.

Intolerance and Bullying

The greatest problem in the world today
is intolerance.
— Princess Diana

Intolerance is a battering ram directed at anyone who is perceived as different and who has therefore become a focus of enmity. You want them to be like you. If they are not like you, you have things to say and you might become enraged, disgusted, and afraid—all of this in the name of like-mindedness.

They, those other ones, become your enemy and the focus of your attention as you rain down your vitriol on their different-from-you selves. They, those other ones, become fair game for your averted eyes, comments, slurs, stares, grimaces, cold shoulders, bullying, graffiti, hate crimes, attacks, thefts, and warheads.

Intolerance is predicated on fear. "Otherness" has scared people for centuries. Wars and conversion missions have been started in the name of homogeneity: *Be like me and then we can understand each other.* Intolerance smacks of fundamentalism: *I'm right, and you're wrong.* It seems there can be no middle ground, and no acceptance of the other.

Many a suicide happens because of this rampage of intolerance. The horror of bullying is a prime example, a universal phenomenon, and it is just beginning to get the attention it deserves.

There are three kinds of bullying: verbal, physical, and social, with verbal abuse being the most common.[16] Bullying includes physical bullying, emotional bullying, and cyber-bullying (i.e., bullying on the Internet, and circulating suggestive or nude photos or messages about someone).

According to studies by Yale University,[17] bullying victims are two to nine times more likely to consider suicide than their non-bullied classmates. A study in the UK found that at least half of the suicides among young people are related to bullying.[18] Further, ABC News reported statistics that showed nearly 30% of students are either

---

[16] Beth Rosenthal, *Bullying* (Greenhaven Press, 2008).

[17] Yale University, Office of Public Affairs, Bullying-Suicide Link Explored in New Study by Researchers at Yale, Yale News, July 16, 2008. http://news.yale.edu/2008/07/16/bullying-suicide-link-explored-new-study-researchers-yale/.

[18] Matt Dickenson, "Research finds bullying link to child suicides," *The Independent*, June 12, 2010. http://www.independent.co.uk/news/uk/home-news/research-finds-bullying-link-to-child-suicides-1999349.html/.

bullies or victims of bullying.[19] Some 160,000 students stay home from school every day because of fear of bullying.

Kids are bullied because they are different, and they can be different in any possible way. If you are different you can be picked on, and you become a potential target. Parents of bullied kids will sometimes go to extreme measures to help their children avoid bullying: one first grader was given plastic surgery to have her ears pinned back.[20]

Kids can be bullied for any number of reasons. Common "differences" that can draw unwanted negative attention include:

◆ having an unusual appearance or body size

◆ showing behaviors of attention-deficit/hyperactive disorder (ADHD)[21]

◆ being diabetic[22]

◆ being gay

◆ being a gifted[23] student

◆ having food allergies[24]

◆ displaying a noticeably high level of anxiety[25]

◆ having learning disabilities[26]

---

[19] Susan Donaldson James, Teen Commits Suicide Due to Bullying: Parents Sue School for Son's Death, ABC News, Health, April 2, 2009. http://abcnews.go.com/Health/MindMoodNews/story?id=7228335/.

[20] Kristin Kane, Childhood Plastic Surgery to Combat Bullying: A Disturbing Trend, Doctors Say, FoxNewsLatino, May 18, 2011, http://latino.foxnews.com/latino/health/2011/05/18/childhood-plastic-surgery-combat-bullying/.

[21] Susan P. Limber, Bullying among Children and Youth with Disabilities and Special Needs. Stop Bullying now! Campaign, 2007. http://www.ldonline.org/article/20001/.

[22] Limber, Bullying.

[23] Sandra G. Boodman, Gifted and Tormented: Academic Stars Often Bullied—and More Likely to Suffer Emotionally as a Result, The Washington Post, May 16, 2006. http://www.washingtonpost.com/wp-dyn/content/article/2006/05/15/AR2006051501103.html/.

[24] Children with Food Allergies Targeted by Bullies. Annals of Allergy, Asthma, and Immunology, September 28, 2011.

[25] G.L. Gladstone, G.B. Parker, G.S. Malhi, Do Bullied Children Become Anxious and Depressed Adults? The Journal of Nervous and Mental Disorders, March 2006. PubMed, http://www.ncbi.nlm.nih.gov/pubmed/16534438/.

[26] Limber, Bullying.

◆ having medical conditions that affect appearance

◆ being obese[27]

◆ stuttering

It's easy to understand that bullying leads to shattered self-esteem, poor self-worth, depression, and suicidal thoughts or actions. Bullying can have long-term emotional ramifications for the victim. Further, a number of school shootings—for example, Columbine—have been caused by bullied kids seeking revenge. Bullying is a symptom of intolerance that escalates and becomes a vicious cycle.

So much suicide is a result of intolerance. Think of all the heartache that is caused by simply not accepting people for who they are and where there are. Intolerance is a mighty powerful belief system. It prevents peace, contributes to suicidality, and causes pain across the globe.

Loss of Relationships

We are social beings. We are hardwired to connect. Relationships give meaning and purpose to our lives. They can be our grandest moments, finest memories, and deepest heartaches. We cannot escape relationships. They are everywhere, and they are part and parcel of our human experience. Relationships are the connective tissue of life. We thrive on them.

Whether with spouse, child, sibling, parent, friend, lover, relative, coworker, or neighbor, life is filled with relationships of varying dimensions, connectedness, and intensities. And when these relationships break or no longer work or seemingly fizzle into nothingness, it can leave you feeling dumbfounded, wounded, and heartbroken.

When a heart is broken, you not only feel alone, you can feel abandoned. And when you feel abandoned, you can feel unlovable and, sometimes, not worthy of life.

The broken heart and the free-fall that ensues following the demise of a relationship can lead to a shattered self that is filled with enormous self-doubt, feelings of unworthiness, and hopelessness. And this, unfortunately, can lead to a consideration of suicide.

---

[27] http://www.cnn.com/2010/HEALTH/05/03/obesity.bullying/.

Isolation and Loneliness

Widowhood, divorce, loss, aging, abandonment, betrayal, shame, poverty, home-lessness, illness, return from military service, and any number or combination of life circumstances can find you alone and isolated. You find yourself disconnected from the world. It's a painful place to be. It's also a depressing place that can lead to suicidal thoughts and actions.

Loneliness contracts a life. There is no one who wants to know what you had for lunch. No one asks you to take something to the post office for them. You are a stranger in your own life, invisible.

In a lonely life, there are precious few relationships of any meaning or consequence. There may be no reason to get out of bed in the morning. Who cares? What does it matter? Your life folds in on itself and gets even smaller. I suspect the energy of your heart shrinks a little as well.

A number of my clients who suffer from serious illnesses are unable to do what they once did socially and professionally. They report that their friends have faded into the distance and their circle of connection has become their medical team. For many in this situation, suicidal thinking is more frequent that you might imagine.

Relationships are not limited to human beings. There are many connections that keep us anchored in the vast river of life. For example, there are connections with your faith or spiritual life, nature, and animals.

Many dogs have given their owner a *raison d'être*. I have had more than one client say to me, in all seriousness, that if it wasn't for their dog, and that wet nose in the morning, they would have taken their life by now. The unconditional love of their dog, and their dog's dependence on them, has kept them alive and on the planet. Recently, a woman told me her parrot did the same thing for her.

Connections of any kind are of primary importance. We all want to feel as if we have value, that we are needed, and that it matters we are here. We need relationships, connections, and what I call tethers—those passions, interests, and causes that engage our minds and hearts and spirits. We also need those small responsibilities where someone or something relies on us. These tethers make us feel alive and a part of something. All of these are at the center of a life fully lived.

When we look at suicide prevention, relationships of all kinds need to be considered and encouraged. Without connection, we become emotionally brittle, closed down, and depressed. And as we know, depression is a primary factor in suicide.

Shame

Shame is a feeling state. It is a deep-down, red-faced humiliation and mortification with oneself. Through the lens of shame, we look at ourselves with complete disgust, revulsion, and contemptibility. We judge ourselves harshly, and show no mercy. We see ourselves as the epitome of gross imperfection, enormous stupidity, complete failure, and abject incompetence. Shame is a powerful force, and it can be a driving factor in suicidal thinking.

Shame is associated with intense feelings of disgrace, dishonor, and condemnation. It is also a major component of ostracism, shunning (think Hester Prynne and her Scarlet "A"), and punishment.

Shame is not the same thing as embarrassment. When we are embarrassed we feel, in varying degrees, uncomfortable with ourselves for something we have done or experienced. We are discomfited by our behavior. For example, we look in a mirror and realize that we had a piece of spinach stuck to our front tooth during our dinner date as we laughed and acted charming.

Nor is shame the same as guilt. We feel guilty when we have violated our personal standard. For example, we forgot to send our favorite Aunt Minnie a birthday card or we didn't check up on a sick friend.

The etymology of the word "shame" is rooted in the words "to cover up, hide." And, that's exactly what we do when we feel ashamed; we want to hide and cover up. We avert our eyes, lower our head, and our shoulders slump. We want to disappear. And when there is intense shame,[28] there is vasodilation (blushing) along with increased body heat and warmth.

Like fear, shame is a learned response. No one is born with shame. Shame is passed along by supercritical parents, relatives, employers, teachers, and the like. They regularly make denigrating comments that make you feel horrible about yourself. You might hear that you are stupid, worthless, unlovable, ugly, fat, a failure, incompetent, and any number of put-downs that attack your very essence. These critical folks (from their own wounded and unhealed hearts) tell you these terrible things about yourself, and you believe them. You unconsciously absorb

---

[28] Some people blush for the slightest attention or situations where they feel judged or evaluated by others. Some suffer from what is called Chronic Blushing or pathological blushing, where they blush first, then feel embarrassed and anxious because they have blushed.

their personal poison and drink it in as truth. You forever feel not good enough, not lovable enough, not *enough* enough. Shame says, *I am a bad person.*

You can feel ashamed when you are stopped for a DUI (i.e., driving while intoxicated); are verbally abused in front of your co-workers; or tell your friends your father died of a heart attack when he actually died by suicide. You can feel shame when you learn you are infertile or you need to file for bankruptcy. You can be filled with shame and the attendant self-loathing after you rage at your children or realize you have sent a scathing email to the wrong person.

Perfectionists, understandably, carry a tremendous load of shame. Members of dysfunctional families where there is addiction, violence, anger, and control issues also live with shame every day of their lives. Shame is all too common in cases of child abuse and child neglect. And, we all carry the secret shame of being ashamed.

Brené Brown, PhD, LMSW, is a researcher and storyteller who studies vulnerability,[29] courage, worthiness, and shame.[30] Brown has discerned what she calls her 1-2-3's of shame:

1. "Shame is universal. It is one of the most primitive of human emotions. The only people who don't have shame are those who have no empathy and lack the capacity for human connection. Here's your choice: Fess up to experiencing shame or admit that you're a sociopath."

2. "We are all afraid to talk about shame."

3. "The less we talk about shame, the more control shame has over our lives."[31]

    Further, Brown has identified 12 categories of shame.[32]

    ◆ Addiction

    ◆ Aging

    ◆ Appearance and body image

    ◆ Being stereotyped or labeled

    ◆ Family

    ◆ Mental and physical health

    ◆ Money and work

    ◆ Motherhood/fatherhood

---

[29] Check out Brené Brown's TED talk, The Power of Vulnerability.
[30] Check out Brené Brown's TED talk, Listening to Shame.
[31] Brené Brown, Ph.D., LMSW, *Daring Greatly* (Gotham Books, 2012), p. 68.
[32] Brené Brown, *Daring Greatly*, p. 69.

◈ Parenting

◈ Religion

◈ Sex

◈ Surviving trauma

Within each of these shame categories, we can see a link to suicidal thinking and behavior. Brown reminds us, "Shame is such a powerful emotion that it can literally overcome us." It can. It does, and, alas, too frequently results in suicide.

Soul Loss

Not all suicides are defined by mental illness, substance abuse, and unrelenting pain. There are many ways in which we see and interpret the world. From time immemorial, the soul, our spark of being, has been viewed as our primary force of life. It is what animates us.

If we have been abused, humiliated, oppressed, terrorized, tortured, traumatized, or hurt physically or emotionally in any powerful way, our soul can be crushed. Our life force leaks out. We are no longer our whole selves. We have lost some of our light and we are hunkered down in a protective, survival mode. If the soul loss is profound, we become numb, hollow, and begin to move through life in a disconnected, zombie-like way. We see profound soul loss in the eyes of our military, childhood sexual abuse survivors, and the severely bullied, to name a few.

Soul loss is also considered a primary cause for suicide. Soul loss does not necessarily preclude the diagnostic criteria, but, instead, often views the diagnostic criteria as further evidence of soul loss.

The Indigenous world has long honored the soul. Illness, depression, trauma, and other Western-labeled maladies are explained as soul loss. If the soul is tended, then the body, mind, and heart can heal.

To explain further, here is an example:

In South America, a young girl is no longer speaking. She has become totally silent. Her parents take her to doctors and specialists, but to no avail. As a last resort, they drive to a village in the country and take their daughter to a local shaman. He tells them to leave their daughter with his tribe for the week. The shaman then instructs the women to bathe the girl daily and, while bathing her, they are to sing her healing songs. At the end of the week, the girl begins to speak and tells of the rape she had recently endured. She had refound her voice and was healed.

I suggest that soul loss runs parallel to psychoneuroimmunology (PNI), which looks at the mind-body (and often, spirit) interaction. Science does recognize that our thoughts and feelings influence our well-being. As a result, we now see more holistic treatments, an awareness of the role of the soul, as well as an acceptance of assorted energy modalities to help bring the individual back to wholeness.

Spiritual Crisis, Karmic Ruts, and Soul Contracts

Spiritual crises refer to the personal relationship with "the God of your understanding."[33] Our thinking is formed with our particular and idiosyncratic concept of God. Is our God benevolent, avenging, paternal, or punishing? We sometimes struggle with our thoughts about God. Are we disappointing her? Perhaps we feel we have grievously sinned, and we don't deserve this gift called *life*. This can lead to great confusion, self-punishment, and even suicide.

If you are open to the idea of reincarnation, you may want to explore the notions of a karmic rut[34] and soul contracts.

A karmic rut is the theory that a soul repeatedly chooses suicide as its default option over various lifetimes when the going got too tough. Ideally, the soul, in its present incarnation, will become more aware and will stay present to work through life's difficulties, for optimum soul growth. For someone in a karmic rut, the pull toward suicide is familiar and strong.

Soul contracts,[35] as the name suggests, are contracts made on a soul level, not the 3D physical level. The contract is intended for soul growth and it might go something like this: "As a soul, I raise my hand and say, "*Yes, in this lifetime, I will experience a loss by suicide. Perhaps this loss will teach me an invaluable lesson about compassion that I need to learn.*" Conversely, "*I will die by suicide to help the souls of my loved ones.*"

Suicide happens for a multitude of reasons and, frequently, a confluence of factors leads to the ultimate choice. We humans are complicated and unique. As we have explored, we are pushed and pulled by genetic and environmental influences, brain injuries, traumas and stressors, substance abuse and addiction, intolerance and bullying, loss of relationships and isolation, soul loss, and more that can lead to suicidal actions.

---

33 Thanks to Rabbi Brian of Religion-Outside-The-Box for that great phrase.

34 Conversation with Joan Pancoe.

35 The concept of soul contracts was introduced to me by Caroline Myss in her workshops during the early 1990s.

You live out the confusions
until they become clear.

— Anaïs Nin

Too many things are occurring
for even a big heart to hold.

— From an essay by W. B. Yeats

Chapter Four

Special circumstances and considerations

Suicide, a Hot Potato

Heretofore, in American culture, suicide has been a taboo topic. Now, it is so headline-making and societally embarrassing that clinicians and researchers are searching madly for answers and trying to quantify criteria.

Suicide is not an easy topic. Because of that, it often becomes the focus of controversy, outrage, and is frequently a political, religious, and moral hot potato. Everyone seems to have an opinion about suicide or the attendant factors connected to suicide, such as gun control, substance abuse, mental health, the role of government in providing social services, end-of-life choices, and the like.

The intent of this chapter is to open windows and explore some of these deeply nuanced and complicated topics without judgment or bias. We want to delve into these issues with an open heart.

To that end, we will take a close look at certain categories, or special circumstances, of people who may be at particular risk, beginning with teens. It is startling to learn that "more teenagers die from suicide than from cancer, heart disease, AIDS, birth defects, stroke, pneumonia, influenza, and chronic lung disease combined."[1] We will consider the high rates of suicide in the military and acknowledge the trauma of first responders. We will also explore the question, "Is addiction a form of slow suicide?" We will put maternal suicide on the table for your consideration. We will look at suicide as an end-of-life option, with several personal stories to illuminate the thinking of those who want their life to end with dignity. And, we will consider the ultimate lesson that suicide teaches us.

Teenagers and Suicide

*"Over 70% of adolescent suicides may be complicated
by drug and alcohol use and dependence."*[2]

The suicide of a young person is tragic. It can feel as if we failed them because they made, or attempted to make, that lethal choice. However, it is not that simple. It is *never* that simple because we are talking about people who, by definition, are going through incredible biological and emotional changes. Their brains are still developing. And, most importantly, teenagers are trying to figure out who they are as individuals, and what their place is in the world.

Teenagers straddle the wobbly bridge between childhood and adulthood. Their hormones are constantly surging, and their emotions reflect that. They are pressured by their peers to fit in, and they want to find acceptance on a group level. As teenagers move away from the family, their first social unit, they go out and explore. Their search and discovery of new social groups may lead them down strange, new paths. They stop, if only for a while, where they find comfortable resonance, and they pull up a chair. They want to belong. Their friends become primary.

And this is how it should be. Developmentally, teenagers need to pull back and begin the process of individuation. This is when they begin to discern for themselves who they are, what they believe, and how they think. After all, these years form the road to their adulthood. And, concurrently as well as paradoxically, our teens want and need to feel that they are still mom and dad's cherished one.

---

[1] National Strategy for Suicide Prevention: Goals and Objectives for Action, 2001, http://www.sprc.org/sites/sprc.org/files/library/nssp.pdf.

[2] N.S. Miller, J.C. Mahler, and M.S. Gold, Suicide risk associated with drug and alcohol dependence, *Journal of Addiction Disorders* 10, no. 3 (1991): 49–61.

As the parents

As adults, we often forget the immediacy of angst that comes with being a teenager. We can forget how it feels to be in a body—as if we were in a werewolf movie—that is constantly morphing, both physically and emotionally. There is the striving for acceptance and the sampling of lifestyles to discover an identity. E-v-e-r-y-t-h-i-n-g feels so important and so necessary at this *very* moment. It *has* to happen now. It is a matter of social life or death. Don't we understand?

And, often, as much as we love our kids, we don't remember that exact feeling—the primal rawness of adolescence and its urgency. Like pioneers in space, we work our way through the virgin territory of their teenage years, doing our best to remember our own youth. We proceed, step-by-step, emotion-by-emotion, always on the lookout for danger. We read books and come to understand that their brains are not fully developed, and that they need more sleep. We also know we want them to be more responsible and accountable. We are proud and worried, panicked and fearful. We second-guess ourselves. Can we trust them? Can we trust our own instincts?

We look for signs to help us read their shifting selves. Are they using drugs, drinking and driving, skipping school, having unprotected sex, flunking classes, or lying to us—boldfaced—as they live their lives like a covert spy with a double life? We want them to get through these tumultuous years relatively unscathed. Everything feels tender and fragile—it could all come tumbling down, any minute, like a house of cards.

Their moods change on a dime. It seems as if we can't talk anymore, or else we have a conversation that connects us one minute, and a few hours later it's like it never happened. We hold our breath, try to be supportive and encouraging, establish those ever-important boundaries, and get answers to our questions. Sometimes, it feels as if we have a stranger at our kitchen table. We worry, oh God, we worry a lot about their safety and well-being.

Being the teenager

Look through the perceptual viewfinder of a teenager, and you'll see their story. They are standing upon a huge world stage that is watching every move and judging, belittling, bullying, accepting, embarrassing, rejecting, heckling, applauding, laughing, shaming, or throwing tomatoes at their nascent psyches. High drama, indeed, and it can hurt like hell.

It is exhausting to fend off real or perceived foes, react to almost every social nuance, and determine who you are in the midst of this upheaval and uncertainty. By definition, you are conflicted. Most likely you are conflicted—in varying degrees, and at various times—with your parents, your siblings, and some of your teachers and classmates. You probably struggle with peer pressure and social expectations. It is not easy to be anchored, much less balanced, when you straddle two worlds.

You might experience bullying. When it is severe, you cannot even hear what the teacher says in class. You are shut down and only want to survive that day. You go out of your way to avoid any and all interactions that might cause personal embarrassment, shame, or misery. You think maybe you'd rather be dead than go to school.

You most likely experiment with drugs and alcohol. Everyone else is. You might like the taste; it makes you feel mellow and kind of cool. You've been to a few parties where you and your friends have gotten really trashed, really fast. There have been some crazy moments, too, and you have had some wild encounters with the opposite sex. You or your friends have gotten scary sick. When you are high, you feel like you are on top of the world and can do anything. You don't have a problem with drugs or alcohol; you just like this stuff. You are certain you do better in the world when you are high. You are willing to try almost anything.

> "I snuck out of the house and met these guys. We drank for a while. The big guy opened his hand and there was a mambo bunch of pills, all colors and sizes. They dared me. I took them all in one gulp."

> "I was hanging with some friends—they're older. We drank a lot of beer, and then we got in the car and took bats and smashed all the mailboxes down the street. The second time it happened, I got arrested."

Exploring sex is part and parcel of adolescence. In today's fast-paced world, younger and younger teens are having all kinds of sex. There is a flammable mix of partying, sexual abuse, substance abuse, peer pressure, sex, and even violence. There is everything from making out to "lipstick" parties (girls wearing lipstick and performing fellatio on boys), to gang rape.

"I was at this party. I was mad at my boyfriend so I got really drunk. Six boys picked me up and carried me behind a dumpster. I remember being carried. They were going to rape me. Somebody saw them and made them stop."

"My friends cheered me on as I chugged the vodka. I am known for holding my alcohol. Later, I woke up naked in a bathroom with scratches and bruises on my body. I want to make believe it never happened. I don't remember anything."

Let's look at the pressures

Given all the pressures, demands, and the rapidity with which young people have adult experiences, it is no surprise—and very sad—that teenagers consider suicide an option when their lives become unbearable. To reach that place of despair and hopelessness, there must be mitigating factors.

Parents are often clueless, because their kids are so skilled at operating under their radar. Parents might say: *What happened? How did things go so wrong, so fast? Why didn't you talk to me? Yes, I probably would have yelled, but we would have gotten through it.*

Let's consider possibilities that could potentially lead to the dangerous tipping point of suicidal thinking and/or doing.

There are three factors to consider:

1. The body-mind realities

2. Nature and nurture influences

3. The confluence of individual stressors

Body-mind realities

Despite some of their adult behaviors, adolescents have age-related and biological factors that influence their ability to problem-solve and make good decisions. These factors are normal, and they influence an adolescent's ability to cope, handle, think, and discern. The life experiences of an adolescent are limited and this shortens their perspective. Further, teens are operating without their full mental bandwidth (again, a developmental reality), and their hormones are pushing their physical and emotional selves to the limit. In other words, their bodies, minds, and concomitant emotions are in flux, and this influences their behaviors.

Their body-mind realities look like this:

◆ Brains that are not fully developed

◆ Emotions that swing high and low

◆ Hormones that influence their feelings and behaviors

◆ Impulsivity and/or the need to do it *now*

◆ Limited life experience

◆ Coping responses that are still developing

These realities are beyond a teen's ability to control or manage, because they are a process of maturation and development. That said, it is always helpful to educate our teens about what is going on with them. This hormonal rampage does not give them a hall pass for crazy behavior. It *can* explain a piece of the cognitive-behavioral puzzle and why some choices are made, such as driving 100 mph down the highway, running away to meet a romantic interest, or becoming wildly furious about a minor injustice that was meted out to a friend.

The nature and nurture influencers[3]

"Nature" is the way your child came into this world—the genetic loading, the biological vulnerabilities, physical attributes, physical and mental strengths and/or impairments, etc. For example, does your child have big feet, near-sightedness, or an aptitude for math or music? This is not something one can control. Relative to suicide, the inherited elements that are important to consider include a family history of mental illness, suicide, depression, and substance abuse.

"Nurture" is the impact of the environment on your child. This is something you can influence. How has your child been raised and parented? Has your child been encouraged and supported? Does she feel safe and secure? Does he have a strong sense of self? What kind of home environment, neighborhood, and community involvement is in place?

The nurture part is particularly relevant when it comes to suicide. Is there positive, modeled behavior? Has the teen been taught, or had to learn through the school of hard-knocks, good coping skills? Is there someone to trust? Are there sup-

---

3 See Chapter 2, Understanding Suicide, and Chapter 3, What Leads to Suicide, for more discussion of nature vs. nurture.

portive loved ones who care and are willing, and able, to take steps to protect, nurture, and guide the teen's well-being?

The nature part of this dynamic cannot be changed. However, it can become a point of awareness. For example, if your teen is the son of an alcoholic, he will be predisposed and genetically wired when it comes to alcohol. He will need to be careful that experimentation does not become a habit that hijacks his brain and body. The scenario is the same if he is the son of a diabetic. It is part of self-care to know your physical vulnerabilities in regard to the potential impact of your inherited make-up.

As we discussed, nurture is an exceedingly important element in this equation. Where does your child feel happy, safe, supported, and comforted? Is it with her friends, her friends' parents, or with you?

When teens have a problem, the first place to assess is the family; the second area is school, both the teachers and students; and the third place is friends. What are the relationships like? Are they healthy, abusive, dismissive, shaming, or fearful? After you explore this, and come up with some answers, then you drill down to the teen's individual and idiosyncratic issues.

Confluence of individual stressors

Every person is unique, and everyone's life is a distinct constellation of circumstances and experiences. Within these unique patterns, we look at individual stressors. For teenagers, these stressors can include, but are not limited to:

◆ Bullying

◆ Chronic lying

◆ Eating disorders

◆ Family problems

◆ Gambling habit

◆ Learning disabilities

◆ Legal problems

◆ Medical issues

◆ Physical disabilities or limitations

◆ The need to be perfect, always

◆ Risky behavior

◆ School problems

◆ Sexual abuse

◆ Sexual confusion

◆ Substance abuse

◆ Trauma

The accumulation of stress—and stress is cumulative as well as additive—can create pain, the enormity of which outweighs the potential for happiness. These individual and idiosyncratic stressors can create an opening, or a place of vulnerability, that may spin a person out of control.

Combine the struggles of adolescence, concerns at home and school, plus the family history, and these stressors can create a breaking point where suicide might be considered and/or acted upon by a teenager.

Because life is complicated, and adolescence can be like a high-speed train with many moving parts, there is usually a confluence of stressors rather than just a single one. Often, one problem leads to another problem. And, keep in mind, the severity of these stressors is significant in the assessment of our teens.

Why is suicide seen as an option?

There is a popular saying that states, "Suicide is a permanent solution to a short-term problem." This is particularly true for teens and young adults who often see the world in black-and-white constructs, feel doomed and option-less in their current situation, and are in dire emotional and mental distress.

For adolescents, suicide can become an option and seem like the answer when:

◆ The pain of their daily life is too much to bear.

◆ They feel totally alone, misunderstood, and/or hated.

◆ They have experienced a cluster of losses, failures, or problems and can imagine no way to get back on their feet.

◈ Everything feels hopeless, stuck, and unfixable.

◈ They are in big, big trouble and see no way out.

◈ They feel their parents don't care or are too angry to help.

◈ They are filled with shame and regret.

◈ Their heart has been broken, and they feel forever unlovable.

◈ The idea of suicide has become seductive.

◈ They want to follow in the footsteps of a classmate.

Needless to say, there is an overlap in feelings and motivations for suicide in teens and adults, because pain is pain.

What makes teen suicide especially difficult to accept is that, as adults, we see the potential of a full life and know that there are (or were) probable solutions to their pain and circumstance. We also know that because they are young, they are impulsive and take risks we no longer understand.

When it comes to younger adults, a tragic end feels exactly that—a tragic end; we adults know there is always a second, third, or, even, fourth act. It feels that their short life was truncated for absolutely nothing, and we are left imagining the person they would have grown into had they lived. We grieve for the possibilities that are no more.

How do we change this situation so that our young people come to know, and fully grasp, that there are options, that they are not alone, and that support is available? An even more important question is this: How do we teach them to value their life and understand the impact of their choices? We want them safe, happy, and alive.

I think many teenagers feel alone and disconnected, without any real support, for valid reasons. Often there is no straight-shooting, truth-telling individual, with both heart and integrity, to remind them why we need and want them to be here on the planet. There is no one to tell them it's important to learn that missteps, screwups, and failures are not only part of life, those actions become the very nutrients in each messy compost heap that results in seeding future success and wisdom.

This business called life is a process. It is not linear, nor is it circular. It is a holographic movement unto itself. We have so many layers—emotional, mental, physical, and creative, to name a few—that need to grow, develop, and expand. It all takes time.

We do see that education about suicide prevention is proving helpful in lowering the rate of teen suicides. The widespread problem of teen substance abuse requires more education, more involvement by parents, lots of communication, and less media influence.

In our stressed-out, success-oriented world, we might consider teaching self-awareness and empowerment to our teens in a way that leads to self-mastery. Here are some possible ways to earn and learn mastery:

◆ Increase communication skills. (Ask for what you need, learn how to say no and create personal boundaries.)

◆ Learn emotional fluency and emotional intelligence. (How to talk about and deal with feelings)

◆ Use expressive arts like dance, drama, journal writing, music, painting, storytelling, etc. (Engage the non-linear side of the brain to express, expand, and feel joy.)

◆ Use mindfulness meditation. (Learning how to still the mind, get grounded in yourself, and be present—that's where the power is.)

◆ Have reverence and compassion for one's self and others in the world.

◆ Develop a deep relationship with nature.

◆ Practice yoga. (All that stretching can relieve a whole lot of stress, and it's a tool you can carry forward.)

◆ Do volunteer service. (To expand perspectives, better understand your place in the world, and experience the gift of service to others.)

Through these suggestions, teens can learn ways to express their thoughts and feelings, connect with others, protect and honor the self, connect with their inborn creativity, quiet their mind, connect with their body, have reverence for the natural world and feel part of it, and expand their worldview. This is all excellent training for our future thinkers, leaders, teachers, and healers who will shape the coming world. (It is also excellent training for future parents.)

a star

a star
a tree
and the longing in between

by Gabriel Rosenstock

The Military and Suicide

Nearly one in five suicides nationally is a veteran. . . .

Veterans are killing themselves at more than double the rate of the civilian population [since 2006, the wars in Iraq and Afghanistan][4]

Suicide was the first leading cause of death for female veterans and the second leading cause of death for male veterans [1993–2002][5]

1 in 5 veterans of the Iraq and Afghanistan wars are diagnosed with PTSD.[6]

Whether you are a veteran, presently serving in the military, or in the reserves, the news reports tell us that there are many among your ranks who are, or have been, suicidal or lost to suicide. This is tragic.

I think being in the armed forces, in service to your country, during times of war, conflict, and increased global aggression, and plunked down in an environment of win-at-all-costs mentality changes a person to the very core. How could it not?

The onslaught of death and destruction, the heartbreak of collateral damage, the extreme emotional and physical duress, and the negligible tolerance for any kind of vulnerability (and, one might wonder, humanity in some circumstances) forcibly wear a person down. Stressful would be an understatement. Traumatic would seem more in keeping with the realities. Most of us would agree that war is hell. And, these days, it sounds like war is a specialized kind of hell with multiple tours of duty, military sexual trauma (MST), and the amped-up fury and aggression of some of your fellow soldiers.

There is a report suggesting that the unknown factor in military suicides—and researchers feel this is particularly evidenced by the number of non-combat soldiers

---

4 Jeff Hargarten, Forrest Burnson, Bonnie Campo, and Chase Cook, Suicide rate for veterans far exceeds that of civilian population, The Center for Public Integrity, August 30, 2013, http:// www. publicintegrity.org/2013/08/30/13292/suicide-rate-veterans-far-exceeds-civilian-population/.

5 Suicide in the Military, http://www.deploymentpsych.org/, Center for Deployment Psychology: Preparing Professionals to Support Warriors and Their Families. The study mentioned is Wiebe et al. 2006.

6 http://www.facethefactsusa.org/facts/the-true-price-of-war-in-human-terms, a project of The George Washington University, School of Media and Public Affairs.

who take their lives—is "the soaring rates of psychiatric drug prescribing since 2003. Known medication side effects of these drugs such as increased aggression and suicidal thinking are reflected in similar uptrends in the rates of military domestic violence, child abuse and sex crimes, as well as self-harm."[7] This may be a factor, but I don't think it is the one and only, much less the primary, factor. Suicide is complicated. Human beings are complicated and carry their individual genetic predispositions, personal history, and reservoirs of resilience.

The military is now linking mild traumatic brain injury (TBI) and concussions with a higher risk for suicide.[8] The soft-tissue damage of the brain is cumulative. Therefore, each repeated incident of a concussion or brain injury increases the damage to the brain and increases the risk for suicidal thoughts and actions. Military personnel are especially at risk for repeated brain injuries.

All soldiers are dealing with the stressors of combat and deployment; some female soldiers are also dealing with sexual trauma within their own ranks. For the female vet, there can be the additional burden of what is now termed military sexual trauma (MST). According to one female vet,[9] it is endemic to military service. Women soldiers are subjected to comments as they bend over during daily exercise. There is running sexual commentary about a woman's body parts and her sexual proclivities. There is leering and peering into the deliberately created peepholes in the women's camp showers. Some of the higher-ranking male soldiers are known to use their positions for sexual favors.

I was told that most female soldiers who had experienced MST would do anything to avoid showing their vulnerability to their male counterparts. They felt it was too high a price to pay. They refused to show that had been broken by the sexual abuse. These women felt isolated, disconnected, and unsafe. They became hypervigilant, waiting for an attack, both from within their ranks and outside the camp.

---

[7] The Citizens Commission on Human Rights, The Hidden Enemy Documentary Exposes the Covert Operation behind Military Suicides, http://www.cchr.org/documentaries/the-hidden-enemy.html?gclid=CNT5vv-P178CFdBi7AodfSMAHg/.

[8] Repeat Brain Injury Raises Soldiers' Risk of Suicide, National Center for Veterans Studies, University of Utah, UNews, May 15, 2013, http://unews.utah.edu/. See also Chapter 3 of this book, What Leads to Suicide? under Brain Issues, for more discussion.

[9] Personal conversations in October 2013.

Sexual abuse, unto itself, is traumatic. Sexual abuse amidst the intensity of combat conditions is an acute stressor that requires attention and healing for the returning female vet.

A study done by National Center for Veterans Studies indicated that "the most frequent reason a soldier gave for attempting suicide was intense emotional pain."[10] That goes without saying, but I think there is more, so much more.

Veterans return home and they are strangers in the place they once called home. They have lived through intense experiences. These intense experiences have created ironclad bonds with fellow soldiers in their units. When the action came, their days were primal, raw, and extreme. They lived on the precipice of life and death, victory and destruction.

The vets come home eager to connect with their loved ones. They try to acclimate themselves to everyday life, to the expectations of family, friends, and society. Yet, rarely do they want to talk about their combat experiences, save with their fellow troop mates. Their hearts have been armored by exposure to the unthinkable and horrific. They retreat inside their heads, not wanting to sully their family with the ravages of combat, preferring to contain the rumbling conflict of feelings and raging aggression within themselves.

Frequently, returning soldiers suffer post-traumatic stress disorder (PTSD). They become disoriented, hypervigilant, pummeled with flashbacks, terrorized, and disconnected from loved ones. They might drink or drug to numb the pain. They might push the envelope and engage in risky behaviors simply to feel, feel something . . . a rush of adrenalin to feel—at least for the moment—they are alive. They may be locked in a cycle of rage and violent behavior. They may hold the thought of suicide in their hands. They are trying their best to survive. It isn't easy and it is even harder to talk about.

They hunker down emotionally—and sometimes physically, too—waiting for the enemy to attack them one more time. This enemy has many faces. It can be the literal enemy they faced, what they witnessed and endured, what they were called to do in the name of duty, or how they judged themselves or were judged by others. And they relive these terrors, often on a nightly basis. They have survived combat, but now they my must win the war within themselves.

---

[10] Joseph Bobrow, Military Suicide, Emotional Anguish and Healing, The Huffington Post, July 20, 2012, http://www.huffingtonpost.com/joseph-bobrow/military-suicide_b_1691148.html.

In his book, *Warrior's Return: Restoring the Soul after War*, Edward Tick, PhD, offers these two poignant examples:

> *A middle-aged father found his 19-year-old son hanging in their basement just weeks after returning from Afghanistan. The son left a note saying he could not live with the memories of what he saw and did in the war. In another family, a husband and wife were both National Guard officers. The husband deployed while his wife waited at home. Upon his return, she deployed. The woman soldier became depressed. Overseas she was put on anti-depressants that were revoked when she left. "We don't want you to go home a medical statistic," she was told. Upon return she committed suicide. Her death was said to be from depression, not PTSD.[11]*

Dr. Tick[12] also writes,

> *In these modern wars many more veterans die from suicide after their wars than were actually killed in combat during them. Troop suicide is "now more lethal than combat."... Many after-conflict deaths result from self-inflicted wounds, accidents, legal or illegal drug overdoses or alcoholism—with no messages left behind. Many veterans die in violent ways after violent service. Accidents—"unconscious suicides"—and criminal activity—"death by cop"—may have military or combat-generated components. Iraq and Afghanistan veterans have a 75% higher rate of fatal motor vehicle accidents than non-vets. They are more at risk in the months following deployment; those serving multiple tours are the highest risk. "Accidental deaths" may mean that the terrible veteran suicide rate is even higher than we know. Nobody can know how many of these incidents are "accidents." [13]*

This suggests that the numbers of military suicides are under-reported and that the concern is bigger—and more heartbreaking—than we have imagined.

---

[11] Edward Tick, PhD, *Warrior's Return: Restoring the Soul after War*, pre-publication pages. Sounds True. November, 2014.

[12] Edward Tick, PhD, is Founding Director of Soldier's Heart: Veterans' Safe Return Programs.

[13] Tick, *Warrior's Return*.

There was a news blurb about a veteran being left for over three hours in a VA clinic.[14] The vet did not have an appointment and knew he would have to wait to get his prescription filled, but was told he would be seen that day. However, he found himself watching people pack up for the day and unaware of his presence. He had been forgotten.

This is emblematic of how many veterans feel. They feel forgotten, not supported, not cared for, not appreciated, and thwarted in receiving what has been promised to them, especially in terms of mental health care. The VA system is beyond muddled; it is broken. There are vets taking their lives by suicide while they wait and wait for the promised mental health care.[15]

The military are our sons and daughters, sisters and brothers, mothers and fathers, who answer our nation's call to serve. They need us to bear witness and to help carry the burden of war.

The following poem, "Sentry," by Kate Dhalstedt, evocatively sums it up best:

> *I look into your soft eyes as you hold up your tattered shield—*
>
> *to keep me from seeing . . .*
>
> *The Beast*
>
> *fangs dripping…*
>
> *and you with nowhere to run…*
>
> *But don't think I can't hear*
>
> *the desperate howl behind your silence,*
>
> *the crashing of your heart on the jungle floor.*
>
> *It is you I really want to see,*
>
> *even when it hurts…*

---

14 Patricio G. Balona, Veteran left waiting alone when Orange City VA clinic closes, The Daytona Beach News Journal, news-journalonline.com, July 23, 2014, http://www.news-journalonline.com/article/20140723/news/140729767.

15 Sy Mukherjee, Some Veterans Are Committing Suicide While Waiting To Receive Mental Health Care from the Government, August 6, 2013, http://thinkprogress.org/health/2013/08/06/2418721/veterans-committing-suicide-waiting-for-mental-care/. For a thorough overview of the problem, see http://www.washingtonpost.com/ blogs/the-fix/wp/2014/05/21/ a-guide-to-the-va-and-the-scandals-engulfing-it/.

I ache to hold your broken heart,

and sing and rock and rest…

So, I keep vigil outside your door…

humming the ancient Warrior Song

all night long.[16]

Military suicides are the result of grave and repeated stress and trauma. They can also be viewed as prime examples of soul loss.[17] The weight of war is crushing and indelible.

No one returns home from battle unscathed.

"My beloved military-police officer spouse chose suicide in 2008 after his health imploded. He was a three-tour Vietnam Vet. He had to kill his mortally wounded best friend and buddy, at his urging because it was too horrid to be taken alive even that wounded. That was also the pact the thirteen in that killing mission/patrol had made. The men knew too well that if captured alive, the torture would be unbearable for the security knowledge they possessed. My beloved could never get past having to shoot his best friend—nor his tasks as a counter-intelligence officer. Forever wounded, scarred — changed."[18]

Ideally, we would have no war and soldier suicides would cease to be. But until there is peace, our soldiers and veterans need our help and deserve our respect. And they need support and assistance to deal with both the visible and invisible wounds of war. For these soldiers and vets, the war does not end when they return home. The war relocates behind their eyes and within their bodies.

The rates of military suicide are alarming, horrifying, and, to me, not surprising given the intensities and horrors these men and women endure in today's world.

A Note about First Responders

First responders, as the name implies, are first on the scene of disasters, accidents, and crises. They are the police, firefighters, EMTs, and paramedics.

---

[16] Kate Dahlstedt, "Sentry," unpublished poem, used with permission and used at Soldier's Heart (soldiersheart.net) healing retreats.

[17] Soul loss is further discussed in Chapter 10.

[18] Email correspondence from Reverend C. E. Brown. Used with her permission.

Every community relies heavily on its first responders to establish order after a crisis or chaos. They are integral to the well-being of their community. They ensure a sense of safety and direction in the wake of tragedy.

First responders are often the first on the scene to witness the aftermath of a suicide. Many experienced police officers report that when they have had to handle a death by suicide, "they describe it as the worst day of their lives."[19] With the increased rates of suicidality, these "worst days" are increasing. Like those in the military, first responders are repeatedly facing the horrific. As a result, many are living with trauma reactions, which, in turn, can increase suicidality.

We unintentionally take for granted those who serve our communities. They, too, are impacted by the ever-widening circle of suicide.

Is Addiction a Form of Slow Suicide?

Like the range of suicidality, addiction crosses a broad spectrum. There are many variations on the theme of addiction. It would be unreasonable to suggest that all substance abuse and addictions are a form of suicide. However, is it reasonable to consider some ongoing, long-lasting addictions as a kind of slow death and, by extension, a form of suicide?

Before we dive into the deep end of the pool, let's define our terms:

Substance abuse is just as the name suggests. It is using a substance—such as alcohol, or a drug like cocaine, steroids, ecstasy, heroine, amphetamines, and the like—repeatedly with deleterious effects. Over time, with repeated frequency and escalating usage, one can become psychologically and/or physically dependent. It becomes difficult to say *No*, and back away from the substance. After this happens, a person's life centers around procuring the substance, using the substance, feeling the impact of the substance, and then figuring out how to finance or finagle access to get more of the substance. The goal is to experience the desired feeling—the rush, the high, the mellow effect—from that particular substance.

When it becomes impossible to stay away from the substance of choice, and it is unfathomable to say *No more*, substance abuse becomes a runaway train. This is addiction: The brain is captured, and there is complete attachment to the substance of choice. *Nothing* is as important as maintaining this vicious cycle:

---

[19] Crikey Independent Media, Independent Minds, July 25, 2014, http://blogs.crikey.com.au/croakey/2014/07/25/focus-on-appropriate-care-and-responses-for-those-bereaved-by-suicide/.

Getting the drugs and/or alcohol → Using →

Feeling the effects → Finagling for more.

Repeat.

It becomes the *raison d'être* for living another day, sometimes for living another hour.

Why do people use?

There are many reasons, including life events, physical and/or psychological pain, and a genetic predisposition, that can lead people to using substances.

Generally speaking, substance abusers and addicts use because they are looking for ways to:

◆ Anesthetize their pain and suffering

◆ Blot out memories and panic related to conflict, trauma, and abuse

◆ Conquer social anxiety by finding a way to fit in with others

◆ Deal with their wounded selves

◆ Endure the bleakness of poverty, disability, homelessness, and dire circumstances

◆ Medicate their anxiety and depression

◆ Put a temporary salve on their fears, shame, failures, low self-esteem, and worthlessness

Substance abuse takes the edge off; it becomes a prolonged maladaptive coping response that can run amuck. It gives users another way to deal with their feelings when those feelings are too painful and conflicted. Simultaneously, substance abuse stops emotional development cold in its tracks, and it puts lives in turmoil.

Addicts are about the here and now, and about the details of getting high: procure substances, crash, repeat. It is a cycle of denial. Their addiction hijacks their lives and turns them into another version of themselves. They are stuck in, and blind to, the loop of self-destruction that impairs mental and physical health, sanity, relationships, and well-being.

In comparison to addiction, why do people consider suicide?

Using a broad stroke, people who consider suicide are trying to:

◆ End the bleakness of poverty, disability, homelessness, and dire circumstances

◆ End their pain and suffering

◆ Permanently blot out memories and panic related to conflict, trauma, and abuse

◆ Put a permanent end to their fears and feelings of shame, failure, low self-esteem, and worthlessness

◆ Relieve and terminate the struggle with their wounded selves

Suicide is intended to be The Permanent Out or, for some, a loud and angry, poignant or pained, call of distress. Suicide is the equivalent of a shrieking alarm bell. Addiction, on the other hand, is a chronic beeping that gets louder over time.

Suicidal people plot, plan, ruminate, consider, make gestures, attempt—all to end the pain and disconnection.

Substance abusers remember when they were clean and sober, or hold that thought as a future promise. The majority of substance abusers do not see their lives in a constant downward spiral of addiction. One day, they will get their act together, but, for right now, they need that drink, that hit, that whatever, that will make them feel better, or, at least, less bad.

How are suicide and addiction similar? Where do they intersect?

1. Pain, in any of its multitudinous forms, is the common denominator for both addiction and suicide. Both substance abuse and suicide can be actions and reactions to avoid real or perceived pain.

2. Both suicide and addiction can be responses to trauma such as war, violence, childhood sexual abuse, etc.

3. Genetics—that is, family histories of suicide, addiction, and/or mental illness—can influence the limbic system vulnerabilities, neurotransmitters, emotional make-up, and sensitivities of both an addict and a suicidal person.

4. Mental illness (especially depression), traumatic brain injury, desperate circumstances, or unresolved grief are frequently components of both suicide and substance abuse.

5. Life stressors exacerbate and complicate the emotional well-being of both addicts and suicidal people.

6. The thinking of an addict and a suicidal person can become altered, skewed, limited, and/or irrational.

   — All addicts exhibit what is called "stinkin' thinking," the circular reasoning to continue to use even when it creates havoc and causes pain and problems.

   — There are a small percentage of suicides, especially by those who are physically ill or infirm, that are well-considered personal choices. They have nothing to do with mental illness.

7. Suicidal folks and addicts may both feel:

   — Anger

   — Anxiety

   — Damaged and/or non-existent self-worth

   — Depression and despair

   — Heartbreak and grief

   — Low self-esteem

   — Misunderstood and disconnected from others

   — Shame, guilt, and embarrassment

   — Traumatized

Remembering that every situation is unique, we can see that suicide, and the whole range of suicidal ideation and actions, is often considerably more planned than is substance abuse. Substance abuse is a chronic progression. It is not well thought out or considered; it simply becomes a way to handle and negotiate life. Suicide is a way—usually a premeditated but sometimes an impulsive way—to end life.

From my perspective, suicide is more of an active state. Doesn't it take courage to end your life? If I put a pillow over your face right now, you would pummel me so that you could get that pillow off and keep breathing. Suicidal individuals swim the waters of so much deep pain that the relief and termination of their pain is greater than wanting to take another breath.

Clearly, there are distinctions to be made between suicide and addiction. However, there is an area of common ground where addiction does resemble a slow form of suicide.

When does addiction look like a slow form of suicide?

◆ The addiction has been chronic and long-term.

◆ The addiction has progressed to a place of major physical and psychological impairment.

◆ The addict refuses any and all offers of assistance.

◆ The addict is resigned to his misery.

◆ The addict suffers from mental illness.

◆ The addict is emotionally withdrawn from loved ones.

◆ The addict is hopeless, self-sabotaging and, frequently, defiant or passive-aggressive.

◆ Despite repeated attempts at recovery, rehabilitation, treatment, medication, including drug antagonist treatment, there is chronic relapse behavior, increased mental intractability, and emotions that are shut down.

It is very tough for a loved one to witness the extreme progression of addiction (anorexia is definitely included in this conversation) that can become a form of slow—and tortuous—suicide.

Maternal Suicide

Suicide is the leading cause of maternal death.[20]

Scene: You are a new mother. You are supposed to be happy, elated, and on top of the world. You're not. Your baby is making you crazy, you're so tired … you can't keep up with the demands. You feel totally out of your depth; you feel unfit to be a mother or even a wife. Your thinking is confused. Maybe it would be better for everyone if you weren't around.

---

[20] Margaret Oates, FRCPsych,Suicide: the leading cause of maternal death, *The British Journal of Psychiatry* (2003) 183:279–281.

Women know that they are impacted by their hormones. They have monthly cycles that they ride with the moon. Their loved ones often know their cycles because of mood swings and changes in temperament.

No one goes into motherhood thinking that her own body, the body that helped create, gestate, carry, and birth life would turn on her, so savagely, so counter-intuitively, so far from the picture-perfect state of motherhood she had imagined.

Motherhood itself is a huge transition and life changer. It is E-x-h-a-u-s-t-i-n-g with a capital 'E'. With postpartum depression (PPD), there is a biochemical switch that ratchets up the feelings of being overwhelmed and exhausted. The baby cries and you cry even more. There is no rest for the weary. Even when you are tired, you often cannot rest because you are on high alert. You want to be there for your new baby, 24/7, so restful sleep becomes a thing of the past.

You are propelled, post-pregnancy, into a teeming vortex of alien moods and feelings. Your moods seem so antithetical to motherhood, and this feels like the biggest injustice of all.

There is shame and anger and worry and fear. There are tears, and more tears. *Why can't I handle this? What can I do? How can I keep my baby safe when I feel so unglued? I am not making any sense. I need help, but how can I tell anyone what I am going through? They will think I am a terrible mother.*

Is it unnatural to shy away from your newborn? Can your baby's cry become a trigger for you to consider doing harm to yourself or your child? It can happen with postpartum depression. It is more common than you think.

Research has indicated suicide due to postpartum depression is the leading cause of maternal deaths. [21] That said, they are often under-reported; infection and blood loss seem to get the headlines.[22] The idea of a mother, the archetype of unconditional love and caring, feeling suicidal is totally contradictory to the usual image of a glowing mom holding her newborn infant. How can a mother hold such conflicting feelings? Clearly, it has to be hell.

Today, there are solutions to relieve the pain, suffering, and potential dire consequences of PPD. There are medications to rebalance a new mom's hormones and

---

[21] Oates, Suicide: the leading cause of maternal death.

[22] Katherine Stone, Is Maternal Suicide Overlooked As A Leading Cause of Maternal Mortality? PostPartum Progress blog, October 24, 2011. See also Oates, Suicide: the leading cause of maternal death.

biochemistry[23] as well as support groups. Women are relational by nature[24] and can benefit enormously by connection with other moms who share their same heart-wrenching challenges.

Suicide as a Conscious End-of-life Choice

In various cultures, and at other times in the world's history, suicide was considered a relatively common part of life and death.

When you were ill, or knew it was your time, you walked into the forest and ate the poison berry, or you walked out onto the ice floe. Or, you might tell the others to go on without you, and you would be left with some food and the fire that remained. The others in your group would head toward their destination, knowing you would not survive the elements or the wildlife. Suicide was a choice, a conscious choice. And it was an accepted part of the culture.

In today's world, suicide as an end-of-life choice raises fears and questions for some and proffers relief for others. Assisted suicide is currently legal in five US states: Oregon, Montana, Washington, New Mexico, and Vermont.[25] Assisted suicide is also permitted in Belgium, Luxembourg, the Netherlands, and Switzerland.[26]

Following are some real-life situations for your consideration:

Will you get me my pistol?

Joan's father calls her into her parent's bedroom. Her father is at the end of his life, very ill, and bedridden. He asks Joan to go and get his pistol from its hiding place. Joan knew her father had bullets in his nightstand table. Joan tells her father she doesn't want to do it, but then she thinks to herself, *What would I want?* Joan retrieves the pistol and hands it to her father, holding her breath and allowing her father the dignity of choice.

---

[23] There has been discussion and research around postpartum depression as a possible precursor to bipolar disorder. Clearly, PPD is a hormonal and biochemical issue that requires medical attention.

[24] Thank you, Stone Center at Wellesley, for the research on women being relational.

[25] Erik Eckholm, Assisted Suicide Now Legal in Five States, *New York Times*, February 8, 2014, http://www.telegram.com/article/20140208/NEWS/302089876/1116.

[26] N. Steck et al., Euthanasia and assisted suicide in selected European countries and US states: systematic literature review. PubMed.gov, October 2013, http://www.ncbi.nlm.nih.gov/pubmed/23929402/.

Ten days later, Joan's father died, but not from suicide. Joan thinks her father opted not to take his life because of the impact it would have on his family.

When the time comes...

Sophia's Uncle Max, her mother's brother, calls one afternoon. He calls to say that his wife has just been diagnosed with pancreatic cancer. She already has Parkinson's disease. Uncle Max, himself, has been dealing with his inoperable cancer and laughingly calls himself a drug addict given the amount of pain meds he needs daily to manage his pain.

The reason for Uncle Max's call is to inform his niece that when his wife's pain becomes intolerable, they will take their lives. Further, Uncle Max needs Sophia to deal with Francine, his sister and Sophia's mother, because she is not open to this conversation. Francine could be a difficult woman and most likely suffers from some mental illness.

A number of months later, Sophia receives a letter from her Uncle Max. "If you are reading this letter now," it says, "know that we have passed." In the letter, Uncle Max and his wife express their gratitude for her, their niece, and share some memories. It is a beautiful letter.

Sophia tells her mother, Francine, who is furious, *How could they do this to me? I never got to say goodbye.*

Francine never forgave her brother.

Is there a pill?

You would never know that Iris is in her mid-eighties. She is an attractive, no-nonsense woman, perfectly coiffed with crystal blue eyes. She is dressed in a stylish black-and-white ensemble with modern jewelry. Her voice is strong, her opinions firm, and her heart large.

Iris grew up in a small Midwest farming town. She describes her first job. At nine years of age, she and a friend pulled horseradish root. With burning eyes, they cleaned and cut the horseradish and filled jars, which they sold for ten cents each. She later took that work ethic and became a schoolteacher.

On a double-date at a dance, Iris met Henry, a sailor. They were paired with other partners who did not dance. Iris and Henry did. Henry said that he knew, right then and there, Iris was the one for him.

Iris's father said that Iris had done some stupid things in her life, but this was at the top of the list—she was going to Japan to marry her sailor sweetheart, Henry. Iris worked a second job as a waitress to earn money for her passage. She and Henry corresponded every day and agreed that if it didn't work out, Henry would pay her passage home.

Iris took a tramp steamer to Japan. She was the only single person traveling amidst a handful of couples. The other women were traveling with $200; Iris had $4 to her name. The voyage lasted two weeks. They encountered two typhoons. Iris was violently ill most of the time.

Iris's instincts were right. It all worked out beautifully for Iris and Henry. They were the love of each other's life, happily married for over 50 years. During that time, they were busy raising kids, building careers, traveling and, later, spoiling the grandchildren.

Seven years ago, Henry died of fast-growing pancreatic cancer. Iris dismantled their family home and moved into an upscale assisted living facility.

Over the years, Iris has faced her share of health challenges, and she has attended the funerals of her fellow residents. Now, the topic of death and dying interests her. She has read many books about the subject, and she even led a workshop at her facility about preparing for death.

During our conversation, Iris pulls out her organizer. She has planned her funeral—she asked her children to pick out their favorite items and mementos, from pictures to furniture. She has everything in place when the time comes.

Iris does not want to linger in pain or with total confusion. She asks, *Is there a pill?* She wonders if she can simply move to one of those states where a physician-assisted death is legal. When the time comes, she would like a pill to simply end her life with dignity—the same way she has lived her entire life.

Iris does not fear death; she is ready. She knows she will be with her Henry once again.

The Lesson of Suicide

Suicide is complicated. It is the result of a confluence of factors that can lead to a final and lethal tipping point, or to the consideration of one.

The loss of a loved one by suicide catapults you into a vortex of heavy and intense feelings. Suicide leaves its mark. Suicide breaks your heart, there is no way around it. Your grief and sadness change you, and you will never be the same. Suicide forces you to recognize your vulnerability. You are emotionally ripped open; there is pain, brokenness, and woundedness—and so much that you do not understand. Life feels as fragile and tentative as spun glass.

You can harden your heart and become rigid and intractable from the constant pounding of grief and pain. Or, the break in your heart can open you more fully so that you can feel and love more deeply. Yes, suicide *can* break your heart wide open, and you may become more attuned and aware of the world around you. As the poet Rumi says, *"Break my heart. Oh, break it again, so I can love more fully."*

Life happens. Any of us can come face-to-face with circumstances and experiences that send us into personal chaos. And, the personal chaos is always exacerbated by feeling alone, adrift, and disconnected. When we find ourselves feeling like a person left without an anchor, tether, or a home base, we trudge off—be it physically, mentally, or emotionally—into a form of personal exile. This holds true for those who take their lives, as well as for those who experience the loss of a loved one by suicide.

These feelings of exile speak to one of the primary issues around suicide: Connection and relationship. I concur with Émile Durkheim (see appendix) that society has a significant role in suicide. Society is our system of social groupings and organization. It shapes our relationships and interactions with each other. How we treat one another as individuals, groups, and countries indicates what we value and deem important. Everything is based on relationships, and It is enormously important how we interact within those relationships, and what our interface is with one another. Societally, there is often an inability to walk in another's shoes, to witness pain or injustice. We turn a blind eye because it is uncomfortable. *He's crazy,* or *She did it to herself.* We can pretend that it is of no concern to us.

But that changes with a wide-open and conscious heart, one that understands and accepts that we human animals are all connected. Imagine the beating of a butterfly's wings in South America that influences weather patterns in North America. When one of us is hurt, all of us hurt. When one of us succeeds, we all succeed.

Suicide reminds us that we are all connected. Emotionally, we connect through sympathy, empathy, and compassion.

Sympathy, whose root words translate as "fellow feeling," is an alignment of feelings with someone else. Sympathy is *I feel sad that you feel sad*.

Empathy recognizes and relates to the pain and emotions that someone is feeling. There is total identification with what the other person is feeling. In other words, you are able to walk in their shoes. You truly feel what it feels like to feel like them. A possible downside of empathy is that you can also take on the pain the other person is feeling.

Compassion is not only the deep awareness and empathy for what a person is experiencing; it is also the wish to relieve the pain and suffering. We are motivated to be of service and alleviate the distress of another. Arthur Jersild[27] has described compassion as "the ultimate and most meaningful embodiment of emotional maturity. It is through compassion that a person achieves the highest peak and deepest reach in his or her search for self-fulfillment." The Buddha taught that compassion is a requisite for enlightenment. And, Thomas Merton said, "Compassion is the keen awareness of the interdependence of all things."[28]

Compassion brings us closer to the idea that not only are we all connected, we are all one. In the Lakota Indian language, the phrase, "Mitakuye oyasin," spoken in unison, ends every single ceremony or prayer. It means, "We are all related." Now, perhaps more than ever, it's important for us to remember this truth.

To my way of thinking, suicide teaches a profound lesson in compassion. When we experience a suicide, we want to understand and, frequently, we have to do something, take some action, try to make some kind of difference. We want our loved one's life to mean something. So, we take our wide-open, still-bruised hearts out into the world. We connect and we try to alleviate a bit of pain, smooth the rough edges of unhappiness, or untangle misunderstandings. In doing this, we come back to life and honor our loved one.

The following story beautifully illustrates the lesson of compassion. This suicide changed a village forever.

---

[27] www.compassion.org/.
[28] www.compassion.org/.

The Last Walk for Water, by Scott Harrison[29]

Meda is a large village of dust and rocks that sits on an Ethiopian plateau and sprawls from north to south over several miles. A steep gorge, equivalent to 100 stories, cuts the village in half. Treacherous dirt footpaths, snaking up and down both sides of the mountains, connect the two sides. Arliew Spring, one of the village's sources for water, is at the bottom of the gorge. There's no bank in Meda, no post office, and no general store. There are no power lines or cellular towers. There's no place to buy a Coke, a bottle of water, or AA batteries. A dozen eggs cost only six cents, and while they are small, they are most certainly organic.

Letikiros Hailu was born in the south side of Meda and inherited an impossibly difficult life from her mother, Chekolech. The difficulties started when Chekolech moved reluctantly to the village 25 years earlier in an arranged marriage. It was bad luck that her new husband happened to live in Meda; she'd heard of the severe water problems facing women there. Yet she had no choice but to follow her parents' wishes, and she obediently packed up her belongings.

Her husband turned out to be a brutal man, beating her daily. When Letikiros was four years old, her mom was done with her husband's abuse. She divorced him with the support of the village elders, shooing him out of town ... perhaps before he could harm her daughter as well.

Letikiros was a special girl.

From a young age, she seemed unwilling to simply accept the fate of an ordinary girl's life in Meda. Her friends and neighbors described her as visionary and unique. She was bright. She was beautiful. She was clever.

Gifted or not, like all girls her age in Meda, most of Letikiros's time was spent walking and waiting for water. Her first walk was at eight years old, and her life would change forever after that moment. She'd now get up early four days a week, grab her clay pot, tie it to her back with a rope, and head to the water source to do her part for the family.

Arliew Spring was the closest source to home, but it involved a dangerous and steep climb down a 700-foot cliff. The rocks were loose and slippery, and

[29] Scott Harrison is the founder of charity: water. This piece, with additional notes and commentary, was previously featured in a charity: water publication and is used with the author's permission. Letikiros's village is a charity: water project.

women had been known to fall to their death on this path. Arriving at the dry ravine at the bottom, Letikiros would have to scramble up over giant rocks to reach the spring, which wasn't much of a spring at all. Only enough water seeped out of the rock to fill a few clay pots every hour, and the source was shared at night by monkeys, whose excrement surrounded the area.

Often, Letikiros would arrive at the spring and wait up to eight hours for her turn. Sometimes, she'd find the line of pots and women so long that she'd have to climb back up the hill and head to the Bembya River for water.

The Bembya River was much farther away. It was three hours to the west, a six-hour round-trip, with an even deeper descent; it also had a much prettier view because the rocky path led toward the foot of the towering Simien Mountains. Although the water wasn't clean, there was no shortage of it and no waiting time—the river flowed freely through the deep gorge. On these long waterwalks with her friends, Letikiros would talk and dream about a better life for the people of Meda.

"Things will be changed for us if we work hard and fight to improve our lives!" she would say.

Letikiros walked four days a week for water and attended school part-time on the other three days. Since there was no school in Meda then, reaching the classroom in a neighboring village was another six-hour roundtrip walk. In order for Letikiros to attend school at all, her mother paid to rent a donkey each week that could carry four pots of water on a single trip from the Bembya River. But there simply wasn't enough money to relieve Letikiros of her water duty altogether, and she quickly fell behind. By the age of thirteen, she had only completed the third grade.

Following tradition like her mother, Letikiros was also given to be married at a young age. But her mom wasn't going to see history repeat itself, and she chose for her 13-year-old daughter a young and handsome priest's servant named Abebe. They were childhood friends, so falling in love was easy. Abebe was thin and tall and walked softly. He had a kind, gentle voice and thankfully bore little similarity to Letikiros's father.

"She was beautiful to me. We were in deep love," he said of Letikiros.

They married at the village church in January, and Abebe moved in with his new wife and mother-in-law. Although most girls in Meda dropped out of school as soon as they got married, Letikiros insisted on continuing her education. Even with another member in the house now, the new and larger family continued to rent donkeys for water so she could attend class. Abebe spent his days serving the priests at the church, earning precious little money. Letikiros spent her days walking and waiting.

In the evenings, they ate together and dreamed about an easier life.

On May 19, 2000, Letikiros set out before dawn for Arliew Spring. She didn't eat breakfast, probably thinking she'd arrive at the spring before most of the others so she'd have a shorter wait. May is the hottest and driest month in Tigray, and when she joined her friend Yeshareg on the path, they traveled down the treacherous hill together.

Upon reaching Arliew Spring, they quickly found they weren't the only ones with the idea to leave Meda before dawn. They waited in line all day before filling up their pots and heading back up the cliff together. They reached the peak around 3 p.m. and, at the place where the road forked, Letikiros said goodbye and took a right turn toward her house. It was the last time Yeshareg saw her friend alive.

No one will ever know exactly what went through the mind of Letikiros in the moments that followed. What is known is that somehow she slipped and fell, smashing her clay pot full of water into small pieces. She must have watched in horror as the water spilled out on the dusty ground and abruptly considered the harsh reality of her situation. More than ten hours of walking and waiting had been undone with a simple misstep.

Those who knew her well believed she must have been overcome with shame.

She knew her mother and sister were at home waiting for the water.

She knew they needed her water to cook dinner.

And now, even the clay pot was destroyed—a valuable asset for the family.

So rather than continue on the path home, empty-handed, the 13-year-old child slipped the rope from the pot through the branches of a tree, then around her neck and hanged herself.

*The heart that breaks
open can contain the
whole universe.*

—Joanna Macy

Chapter Five

Was there a note?

Types of Notes

*W*as there a note? It is one of the first questions we ask. We want to know if there were any final words. We look for the link, the connection, the understanding of what has just tragically ended. *Please talk to us one more time.*

Some researchers say that one in six suicides leaves a note.[1] Others estimate that 25% to 33% of the time a suicide is accompanied by a note.

From my interviews with both survivors and those who have attempted suicide, I have concluded that there are four general categories of a suicide note:

No note

Frequently, there is no note.

To the surviving loved one, it can slap like an "F" you. It can feel cold and unfeeling, mean and cruel. It leaves uncertainty. *Did they mean to do it? Was it an accident? Do they want to punish me? Do they really hate me?*

---

[1] M. Gelder, R. Mayou and J. Geddes, Psychiatry (Oxford University Press, 2005). http://en.wikipedia.org/wiki/Suicide_note/.

Or … *Did they just not know what to say or were too ashamed to say it? Was their thinking so scrambled or the focus so skewed? Did they think we wouldn't care?*

One family said, "There was no mental illness. There was no note. We have no peace. We have no resolution." They were left with the eternal, "Why?"

In discussing suicidal attempts with various people, they have offered different perspectives about leaving a note:

One will tell you that he didn't know what to say to his children. It was too overwhelming to put anything into words. He felt so guilty for what he was about to do, there was no way he could compose a note, much less physically write the words.

Another woman said that it never crossed her mind to leave a note. She didn't think it would matter to anyone. Who would care if she was dead?

Another said he was so tired; he was certain that everyone in his family understood his plight. There was nothing more to add.

Another allowed that her family would be better off without her, and a note was not necessary. She wanted them to forget her as fast as possible.

No note, but there is a symbolic message

There are times when there is no note, but there may be symbolic messages left behind for an observant loved one.

For example, a suicide may occur on an anniversary. One man attempted suicide at his mother's grave on the anniversary of her death. One woman took her life on the anniversary date of her daughter's death—her daughter who had died the previous year after a long battle with cancer.

Another man left a particular poem in his journal. It was on the table near the spot where the gunshot rang out. Another left a Bible opened to a passage that was resonant with his situation.

One man used his father's gun, the very gun that his dad had used, to end his life.

In her memoir, Deborah Chamberlain remembered, "It suddenly struck me. Michael *did* leave me a note. In fact, he left a number of them where they could be found. They were his poems and writings about our walks, about the day we went fishing. He wrote about how he felt, so I might understand. He put my name on them so I'd know they were from him to me. Chance, destiny, fate, God's plan, karma, luck, perfect alignment of the stars, providence all worked in harmony so that I could have a part of him forever—his words reflecting our love."[2]

The "best" note, given the circumstances

When it comes to suicide, this is the kind of note we read about in books or see in the movies. It is the note written by a person who is fully aware of his choice and, also, aware, to some degree, of the impact on a loved one. These kinds of notes are meant to be reassuring and helpful. And, they can be.

These notes usually say, "It's not your fault." They often say, "I love you," and possibly, "Please forgive me."

The note may also go into greater emotional "housekeeping" kinds of details with reminders and bequeaths. For example, *Please take care of my mother and help her get through this. Don't forget to give the dog his special medicine. I want you to have that diamond and sapphire ring in my jewelry box—I know you have always liked it. Please take my father's watch in my top dresser drawer.*

One brother understood his recently deceased brother very well. He went to his brother's home office, guessed his passwords, and discovered a journal that explained what had transpired in his life. Then, the family understood the terrible stressors that led up to his brother's suicide, and it provided them with a modicum of relief.

The note full of gibberish

Many people that I spoke with used the same exact words: "The note was full of gibberish." It made no sense. It said nothing.

A note of gibberish suggests the internal chaos of the individual and is usually a result of profound mental illness. The person's thoughts are disorganized and incoherent; their internal processes have run amok.

---

[2] Deborah Chamberlain, *The Orange Picnic* (Courage Publication, 2009), p. 183, ISBN #9780982163801.

That said, one woman wrote a deliberate note of gibberish because she was so angry with her parents for the years of abuse she had endured, and she wanted them to suffer.

Research Findings

Most of us value research and its outcomes. It gives us something tangible to consider, especially in the very intangible and complicated world of suicide. Research can affirm our thinking, surprise us with results, and/or assess volumes of material in a succinct way.

Such is the research on suicide notes by University of Utah professor and researcher, Lenora Olson, PhD. She has identified the most common reasons people do or do not leave a suicide note:

The most common reasons people write suicide notes are:

◆ To ease the pain of those known to the victim.

◆ To increase the pain by creating guilt.

◆ To explain the reason(s).

◆ To express thoughts and feelings not expressed or clearly understood when alive.

◆ To give instructions of disposal of remains.

◆ To confess some other offense like murder.[3]

The most common reasons suicides do not write a note:

◆ They are focused on the practicalities of what they are about to do, such as loading a pistol or tying a noose.

◆ Their choice was impulsive, or at least hasty enough that no time was available to compose a suicide note.

◆ They have nothing to say and/or nobody to say it to.

---

3 Lenora M. Olson, PhD, The use of suicide notes as an aid for understanding motive in completed suicides, thesis, Dept. of Health Promotion and Education, University of Utah, 2005.

◈ They feel that they cannot express what they wish to say.

◈ They do not wish to write about their choice or see no point in doing so.

◈ They are illiterate.

◈ They hope the suicide will be seen as an accident or homicide, common among those who wish to be buried in consecrated ground, or those who hope their families will collect insurance.

In Dr. Olson's research among the suicide notes of Native Americans, Hispanics, and Anglos, she reports that five categories emerge as the most common motivations to take one's life:

1. Feelings of alienation

2. Feelings of failure and inadequacy

3. Feeling psychologically overwhelmed

4. The desire to leave problems behind

5. Seeking reunification with another in an afterlife[4]

These common themes make sense and, perhaps, can offer some comfort in coming to terms with your loved one's suicide.

And common themes notwithstanding, every suicide and suicide note is a unique and individual expression, as you see in the following story.

Sally's Story

Sally and Pete had found each other. It was the second time for both of them. This time, they both felt like they had hit the jackpot. They simply loved being together and enjoyed their small adventures, like traveling to the shore for lunch or even playing toss in the grocery store. It was always fun, always a good time. Pete lived in the here and now. He was playful and spontaneous. He was Sally's best friend.

---

4 Lenora M. Olson, S. Wahab, C. W. Thompson, and L. Durrant, Suicide Notes among Native Americans, Hispanics, and Anglos, *Quality Health Research*, June 17, 2011, doi: 10.1177/ 1049732311412789.

In 2001, Pete was diagnosed with prostate cancer and underwent a radical prostatectomy. Pete never wanted to know the details of his medical condition; he focused on getting better and had Sally act as his point person. Sally researched his illness and did everything she could to keep Pete healthy and alive. The doctors finally convinced Sally to accept and believe that Pete could live a long life, given that his type of prostate cancer was slow growing.

In the fall of 2005, Pete discovered a sore in his mouth. The dentist sent him to an oral surgeon, who, in turn, scheduled Pete for a biopsy. The oral surgeon was vacationing when the pathology report came in. The pathologist called Sally and said, "What are you guys doing? You can't wait. Your husband has stage 4 oral cancer."

Sally was furious. Totally enraged. Pete had been smoking cigarettes on the side. She didn't know. She was madder than hell at what he was doing to her and the kids. He was destroying his life as well as hers.

They were referred to a specialist for surgery. The surgery was botched. Pete left the hospital with an infection. There was chemo and radiation and a refer-ral to an amazing doctor in New York City. There were more surgeries. They cut open Pete's jaw and neck to take out the infection; they stripped muscles from his chest and wrapped and packed them into his neck for his body to absorb and fill the spaces where there had been infection. His neck was like raw meat. Over and over, there were surgeries—and there were infections. Through all of this, Sally had the utmost confidence in Pete's doctors and knew they were doing everything in their power to save his life and restore him to health.

Sally learned how to dress and change his wounds with special gauze pads and sterile gloves twice a day. She dealt with doctors, as Pete never wanted to know the nitty-gritty. He was focused on beating the cancer.

Sally had returned to work when Pete got sick. She never missed a day of work. She couldn't. She used her vacation days for surgeries.

There was unbelievable stress. "I wanted him to live. I wanted my life back. I did everything I could. My emotions were all over the place—I loved him with all my heart and soul, but at the same time I felt betrayed and was so full of anger because Pete continued to smoke after he had been diagnosed with prostate cancer in 2001. I totally believed he had quit. I had been working so hard to help him beat the prostate cancer that when the oral cancer diagnosis was delivered, I felt like I had been punched in the stomach. I had been fighting for his life and he was destroying his life with smoking behind my back." It took a tremendous toll on them both.

In the summer of 2007, Pete realized he couldn't beat it. He had no quality of life. He had already undergone several major surgeries, and more were on the horizon. He wasn't going to live this way and be a burden to his family. Pete started talking suicide. Sally would hear nothing of it. This was too painful. Sally had lost her dad to suicide.

Pete took his case to the Ethics Committee of the hospital, and they ruled he could stop the feeding tube and refuse any artificial feeding methods.

Sally was beside herself, stressed, and furious with Pete. "It was hard enough watching him die." Pete was unable to eat or drink anything from March 2006 until he died in September 2007. During the last few months of his life, it became increasingly difficult for him to talk; in fact, Sally's nerves were so raw that it became difficult for her to understand what Pete was saying.

"We resorted to having Pete write out his part of the conversation and I would answer him. My nerves were shot. I had a hard time focusing and was fighting for my own survival. I was not in a good state of mind. At times, I was a total witch with him. I couldn't eat. I was taking care of Pete, doing the best I could while working full time. I didn't know which way to turn. I just wanted off the merry-go-round and a return to normalcy. I wanted my husband and our lives back!"

Another surgery was scheduled for early October, 2007. It was Labor Day weekend, Pete was home that Saturday, and Sally was working. Normally, Sally's daughter would stop by unannounced to check on Pete. However, that weekend the kids were away. When Sally got home from work that day, there were notes on the doors.

Pete had left identical notes on both the front door and garage door: STOP. DO NOT COME IN. CALL THE POLICE. Sally knew immediately and ran to her neighbor's, banging on the door, telling them to call 911 and saying, "Pete killed himself. I know he killed himself."

The police arrived. They took Sally's door keys, opened the front door, and her dog came flying out of the house. The police cut Pete down and put him on a stretcher. (Pete had used the most vulnerable part of his body—his neck with the tracheostomy opening and skin grafts—and hanged himself. He had been hanging there awhile.)

Sally was told that Pete was conscious and still alive, but the scene was too gruesome and they would not let her see her husband at that moment. They medevac'd Pete to the hospital. He flat-lined in the helicopter, and they brought him back to life. When Sally arrived at the hospital, she fully expected that Pete would be awake. It turned out he was on life support. The hospital kept Pete alive for another day so that the kids could make it home to say their good-byes.

When Pete died, Sally had so many emotions she thought she was going to die. Her weight had plummeted to 102 lbs. Sally was furious with Pete for taking his life. How could he? Sally was at a full boil, full of fury and deep despair following Pete's death. She spent the next year living her life on autopilot, going to work, eating meals over the sink, walking the dog when necessary, and retreating to her bedroom. There was precious little relief.

For a solid year, every day, Sally looked for a note from her husband. "I thought he died hating me because of everything we had gone through. I was a witch, fighting for my sanity. My pregnant daughter needed a biopsy in July, and that was two weeks of torture. There was so much going on. "

One year to the day after Pete's death, Sally was in the garage, getting ready to do yard work. She noticed a police car driving around the circle of her street. She knew they were there for her. Sally went to the front of her house and there was the police car.

Chris, the police officer, told Sally that something told him to get the note and come today. "If you don't want it, I won't give it to you."

Sally said, "I've looked for a year for a note. I thought Pete died hating me for everything I said and my inability to maintain my sanity throughout our ordeal." Of course, she wanted the note.

Chris handed Sally the original note that Sally never knew existed.

Sally couldn't read the note by herself. She read it with her daughter. Pete had written paragraphs to everyone—Sally, the kids, neighbors, favorite aunts, uncles, and cousins. He said it was his time to go. He told the kids how proud he was of them and reminded them that "Mom will need you now." He thanked the neighbors for their help and support; he told anecdotes of happy memories with his relatives. And to Sally, Pete told her he loved her, he was sorry for all the hurt and pain. He apologized for his stupidity in smoking. And, if there is another side, he said he will be there waiting for her.

Given her initial rage, Sally later said that if she had found that letter when Pete had first died, she would have torn it into a million little pieces. Now, his note is very precious to her, and she is so thankful for it.

"My husband gave me the ultimate sacrifice: he killed himself so I could live. I owe it to him to live. It took me a long time. I was not sure I wanted to live. Now, I look forward to life…never thought I'd say that. There is happiness beyond it all. You have to want it and you have to work for it."

Suicide Notes—Voices from the Past[5]

The sadness will last forever.
— Vincent Van Gogh

*I am now about to make the great adventure. I
cannot endure this agonizing pain any longer. It is
all over my body. Neither can I face the impending
blindness. I pray the Lord my soul to take. Amen.*
— Clara Blandick, age 82,
Auntie Em in The Wizard of Oz

*I feel certain that I am going mad again. I feel
we can't go through another of those terrible times. And
I shan't recover this time. I begin to hear voices.*
— Virginia Woolf

*I must end it. There's no hope left. I'll be at peace. No
one had anything to do with this. My decision totally.*
—Freddie Prinze, actor

To my friends: my work is completed. Why wait?
—George Eastman, founder of Eastman Kodak

*My pain is not caused because I am gay.
My pain was caused by how I was treated
because I am gay.*
—Eric James Borges, part of the suicide note
from a gay, teen filmmaker

---

5 www.wikipedia.com, http://en.wikipedia.org/wiki/Suicide_note.

Chapter Six

Tales from the front lines: Survivor stories

The Healing Power of Bearing Witness

From our earliest beginnings, we have shared our stories, dreams, and fears in small tribal groups or clans. A clan gathered around the fire, encouraging their visitors and returning members to relate their adventures and discoveries to the group. People listened to and learned from tales of defeat, survival, and bravery. And so it is, or should be, today. There is nothing more potent or powerful, and potentially healing, than bearing witness to individual experiences. It is an unrivaled education.

In "Tales from the Front Lines," you will read survivor stories about how eleven individuals have dealt with the indescribable aftermath of a loved one's suicide. You will learn how they took that experience and transformed themselves, helped others, or came to a new world-view. Their stories are amazing. From the depths of despair, these individuals were able to find a new baseline, a new way of being.

The stories here offer hope and promise to those who have lost a loved one to suicide. They remind survivors that they can walk through this pain and find themselves again. Admittedly, it is not easy, and it is only possible over time. For only over a period of time can healing—and the perspective to create life anew after grieving such a disastrous death—happen.

Some of those who stepped forward in "Tales from the Front Lines" preferred to remain anonymous, primarily because they did not want to cause more pain for family members. Their stories are either anonymous or told with a pen name. Where real names are used, I have appended "as told by" if the story was shared with me orally, and "by" if the individual has written the story themselves.

The openhearted generosity of the many individuals with whom I spoke and corresponded over these past few years have deepened me in ways beyond words. I am extremely grateful to have shared such intense and intimate experiences. These perceptions and perspectives have not only expanded my thinking, they have widened my heart as well.[1]

The stories in both "Tales from the Front Lines" and the chapter "The Bridge Not Crossed" are the heart and soul of this book. I am certain they will touch, inform, and inspire you.

Prelude

It is said that every suicide leaves six people in its wake.[2] And, each person has his or her own experience of grief and loss.

"Tales from the Front Lines" are stories from people who have survived the loss of a loved one by suicide; they have taken that searing ball of pain and confusion and used it as a catalyst for a new way of being.

In dealing with the myriad of emotions that suicidality evokes, our "front liners" have chosen expressive ways to deal with their pain. Be it a conscious or subconscious drive to reclaim some kind of emotional equilibrium or sanity, each chose not to stay stuck or frozen. Each looked for release and healing in education, the expres-

---

[1] Every conversation I had with these individuals has been woven into the fabric of this entire endeavor. While not every story made it into the book, my correspondents will find themselves echoed in Chapter Seven: Shared Wisdom and the "Survivor Wisdom and Advice" and "How Did you Cope?" pages. Each conversation and personal journey has enriched my thinking and expanded my perspectives. I take full responsibility for any errors, omissions, and any misunderstandings. My apologies if I have unintentionally offended anyone; clearly, that is never my intention.

[2] U.S. Suicide Statistics (2001) estimate, cited by Suicide.org: http://www.suicide.org/suicide-statistics.html.

sive arts, mind and body therapies, movement, support groups, faith, social media, and "paying it forward."

We learn from each other. There is solace and comfort to be found when sharing our life experiences with one another. In full or in snapshot form, here are eleven tales of survival and wisdom.

Two Weeks before Christmas

I lost my 16-year-old son to suicide, and although it was in 1984, it seems as though it was yesterday. It was an unexpected and violent end and will haunt me the rest of my life that I didn't see the "signs"—or that I did see them and just didn't recognize them as being anything other than teenage angst.

Afterward, my husband and I felt anger toward him and toward ourselves, and didn't know how to deal with it; nor did my daughter, who was only 12 at the time. We all felt helpless and we felt shame. Our friends, neighbors, and co-workers didn't know what to do or say to make anything different or better, and some eventually stopped calling or coming by. Most people don't want to talk about the realities of body-bags, blood patterns, police evidence, or other upsetting things. Even some of my daughter's lifelong friends, teachers, and schoolmates pulled away from her.

The only thing that really helped us was trying to establish a pre-event atmosphere of normalcy—as normal as anything could ever again be after the horror of his death. Animals to feed, neighbors that called to check on us when they hadn't seen us lately, co-workers who made me eat ice cream at work because I was losing weight, a new school for my daughter where the kids didn't stare at her, laundry to do, grass to cut, and friends who helped us pack up and move into a new house. Getting a Christmas tree a few days after his death probably seemed weird to some, but not to us. It's all about embracing the small things again after being overwhelmed by the biggest thing you can ever imagine.

The most hurtful comments were probably unintentional and not meant as unkindly as they seemed at the time. Statements like from the co-worker who told me it was because I worked and didn't stay home with him, or people telling us he was in a better place, or that if we'd not had a gun in the house, it never would have happened. Or those who invented and circulated stories of what led up to it or how it was carried out. And the people who quickly ducked their head and pretended they didn't see us in the grocery store.

Does it bother me to talk about it now? No, not really, because it was a long time ago and we've all done a lot of healing. My husband and I are still married, against all odds, and my daughter is grown with a husband and two boys of her own now approaching their teens. Life is good and we're happy. But we are different than we were before it happened. And I cannot drive by the house where it happened without my minds-eye being transported back. Again I can see the crime scene photographer's flash in my son's bedroom window, as I sat in the detective's car on that December night reeling in shock at what had just happened. Worse yet was knowing that my daughter had just lost the innocence of her childhood—all with a single shot.

Mom and Saturday Fudge, as told by Risa Ruse

*O*ne Saturday morning, when Risa was eight years old, she discovered that her mom had made fudge. This was a very unusual event, one reserved only for special occasions.

On this same Saturday morning, Risa's mother told her daughter that she had purchased two airplane tickets—one for Risa and one for her younger sister. The girls were going to California. Risa was told that she would need to call a cab to take Risa and her sister to the airport. The girls were then to fly across the country to live with their grandmother.

Eight-year-old Risa was very confused and upset. She told her mom that she didn't know how to call a cab, much less do anything else that her mother had asked of her. Risa's mother was surprised and frustrated at her daughter's response. She reconsidered and told Risa, "Never mind."

It took a few more years for Risa's mother to complete what she had intended that Saturday morning—and had attempted several times previously—before her actual death at age 30.

Risa was at her first party, a Halloween party, when the call came. She went home and found police cars everywhere. (She and her younger sister, who was nine years old at the time, lived with their mom and her boyfriend.) It was her sister who heard the thump as her mother hit the floor after shooting herself in the head with a rifle that hung over the bed.

At age 11, Risa lost her alcoholic mother to suicide. Risa went into shock. The aftermath was the worst. She became numb; her heart erected walls. It took ten years—her wedding day, to be exact—before she discovered joy again. Risa cried and cried with happiness on that day. She now had a family of her own.

Risa says she has found peace and relief in three ways:

1. Her faith and belief in Jesus has sustained and held her.

2. She uses creative expression to help heal her childhood trauma. She writes rhyming poetry and teaches poetry workshops designed to heal without reliving the trauma.

3. Further, Risa discovered an applied kinesiology-energy body work that has helped to dissolve the layers upon layers of walls around her heart. More recently, she has been accessing the Universal energy through Kundalini Reiki and Qigong to help her further heal and dig out long-standing emotions. Each, in its own way, has helped and continues to help Risa to release the emotions stuck in her body. This work has helped her move forward emotionally in her life and create some peace within her. She says she is very grateful for all the varieties of healing in her life.

Later, I asked Risa about fudge. She said she does not normally eat fudge, but "Today, I ate a piece of my birthday cake. The frosting tasted a little like fudge and I remembered 'her' when I ate. Funny you should ask. I love my mom and miss her while trying not to think about all the past and keep pushing forward. Happy days are here again."

He Was Going to Kill Me

*I*t was intended to be a murder-suicide.

Jim came home from work and pulled his pistol out of the nightstand and aimed it at his fiancée, Stella, who said, "You are not going to shoot me." Jim replied, "Why not?" Stella responded, "Because you love my mother too much and this would hurt her."

Jim, then, turned the gun on himself and shot himself in the head. He later died in the hospital. Stella witnessed it all; she was four months pregnant with their son. They were to be married in a few months.

Stella never returned to their apartment. Her friends pulled out the bloody rug and replaced it. She never told the landlord.

Jim's family and friends were unaware of the extent of Jim's mental health issues, which included a bipolar diagnosis. They turned on Stella and demanded, "What did you do to him?" Stella became an outcast and was seen as the cause of Jim's suicide.

Months later, Jim and Stella's son, Gabe, was born via a C-section. Stella cried non-stop throughout the day of her son's birth. This was not the way it was supposed to be. She was heartbroken. Stella stuffed her pain and rebuilt her life. She remarried and brought a second son into the world.

Yet, as her firstborn son, Gabe, grew and developed, it became clear that he had inherited many of his father's mental health issues plus the in utero *trauma when his mom witnessed Jim's suicide. Gabe's issues made Stella very vigilant.*

When Gabe turned 18 years old, the psychiatrist suggested that it was time for Stella to tell her son the truth about his father's suicide. This brought her son some relief. Gabe promised his mom that he would never take his life. He had seen what it has done to his mom.

Stella says, "I have learned a lot from Jim's death. I learned that mental pain is very real, and I recognize it now when I see it. Until you can actually experience it firsthand, I think we have a tendency to treat it like we ourselves would. If we can deal with the stresses, then the other person should be able to also. I look at people who suffer with PTSD, and I am sure people wonder why two people can go through similar experiences and one suffers and the other doesn't. We are made with different tolerances. I can now spot the difference between someone who is having a hard day and someone who is really struggling. I can tell by the look in my son's eyes when it is serious and when it is just normal."

"I have learned to listen—really listen—even when what I am hearing is hurtful, terrifying, or unpleasant. Listening without reacting, without judging, without supplying an answer (which always seems obvious to me but not to them.)

"I am not brave but I have learned to be vulnerable. Nothing matters in this world as much as the people you love and helping others that are put in your path."

Son, I Won't Come to Your Grave, by Diana deRegnier

For twenty-three years I have grappled with my identity as a mother of a son who took his own life. I am also a woman, a sister, a child, a writer, an activist. I have met many life challenges, yet the scars and weight of the loss of my son make other assaults on the body or soul insignificant in comparison.

It is very hard for others to listen to someone stuck in the anguish of losing a child and doubly so when there is insatiable anger and guilt at ourselves and others, and when we aren't yet reaching for peace because we think we have to do something about the anger and guilt in order to be worthy of healing. In my journey, I had to decide I wanted healing and peace and love even if I don't deserve it; I cannot live in the vomit of my son's suicide.

All losses of loved ones are inhumanely cruel, and suicide comes with an extra-large bottle of the toxins guilt and anger which some of us feel obliged to drink again and again—it never does empty. Some of us have an insatiable need to see everything, talk about the loss, to examine each aspect, to learn every detail of our child's life that we can. And then many of us stay stuck in experiences of sorrow, disappointments, regrets, guilt, and anger. We may move so slowly through the totality of our story that no one, including us, can discern change within us.

When my son died, it was extremely important for me to see, hear, touch, and feel what happened from all available angles. I've done that now. I understand and know all I need to know of the circumstances. With work and self-tolerance, I finally arrived at the point where even without every detail, I see the large picture and each snapshot available to me, and let the rest go.

Not every parent of a child who suicides will feel this way, but when we do, it is excruciating and so rare to find the support of someone who will stand on the shore as we trek through neck-high muck. In addition, some parents whose child did not die by suicide will go through similar angst. For each soul has its own challenges.

Now, I have put the memories of my son's death, linked with a part of my own death, into a secret room for which I hold the key—to lock myself out as well as others. I may enter for moments, or I may crack open the door to remind myself of some item or to grab something in there and retreat. I enter with great caution and do not immerse myself in the totality of that room.

That room is polluted with toxicity and danger. The evils of suicide beckon. Our children were not evil; they were poisoned by real and imagined demons in the harshness of life. They were seduced by suicide.

Greg Furth, author of The Secret World of Drawings: Healing through Art, said to me that my son did not commit suicide; suicide took him. My son became addicted to the idea and immersed himself in a romanticism of suicide. "Suicide ideation" professionals call it, but for me, giving something a catchy idiom turns it into a cliché that doesn't do a suicide victim justice.

So much belongs here in between the beginning of my journey and where I am now, but what I want to tell you is that there came a time when I could no longer willingly jump into the well of despair—what a small word for what I feel. The climb out was killing me and nothing had changed when I reached the top. I was still in anguish and only more weary. I felt no relief. I felt no resolve.

In 1991, I wrote a note to my son on the anniversary of his death that explains some of my crossing:

Dear Son,

I won't come to your grave today

I won't do that to me.

If you have any kind of existence

You know the pain of my loss is always with me.

I don't need to hurt more today

Though I can't help it

My rational mind and my heart are not in sync

My subconscious won't let me forget that this is the day I lost you

Flashes of memory and dreams of horrors come unexpectedly.

But your grave doesn't offer solace

It only tempts me to follow

So if I'm going to live

In protest of the choice you made

If I'm going to see my life to its natural end

And fight my demons rather than lie down for them

I won't come today.

I'll go somewhere that comforts and strengthens me

In honor of you

The you that was music and beauty and genius and life

And in compassion for the beaten spirit who took your life

I will not condone your grievous error by following

I will keep reaching for life

And seeking its treasures with whatever strength I hold within.

All my love,

Mom

His Great, Short, Happy Life

John was a happy, normal, and high-achieving son. He made outstanding grades, was a state diving champion, could sit at the piano and play anything, and attended an Ivy League college where he excelled in economics and physics.

John seemed to have it all, until things began to unravel during his senior year in college. At age 21, John was diagnosed with schizophrenia.

After graduation, there was travel, graduate work, a suicide attempt, and medications that stopped the incessant voices that told John there were implants in his brain and the FBI was in hot pursuit.

The meds also dulled his ever-busy mind and dramatically changed John's personality. He was not the same person anymore. Something profound was lost.

One day, John walked in the house and said, "Hi, Mom," grabbed a yogurt out of the fridge, and said, "Bye, Mom," as he headed out the door. Later that day, John took a high dive off the upper level of the George Washington Bridge in New York City and ended his life. Given his diving background, it was an understandable choice for him.

The police arrived at the door of John's family home that night. Someone had seen him take the dive, and the police had found his abandoned car. His body was discovered several weeks later. John had his wallet on him and he left no note. His mom knew that it was about John when the police came to her door. John was 24 years of age. His mom says John had a "great, short, happy life."

Paying it Forward, by Carl David[3]

*I*t was 1965 when Carl's brother took his life at age 22—leaving no note, giving no signs, much less any warning. The family was left to mourn with no answers.

Carl remembers, *"I was just 16 years old. The effects on myself and my family were devastating, beyond description. We had but two choices: to pull together or tear each other apart. We chose the former and used every bit of strength to rebuild our lives. The challenges were monumental as every day was day one. We had to start over with each sunrise because the aftereffects were so persistent and the pain so ever-present that, at times, it seemed insurmountable. We wondered if we would ever be able to move forward and regain some semblance of life. We realized after a period of time that life does go on, with us or without us, and we had to forge on and live for ourselves and for my brother. He'd have wanted that and we knew that whatever the cause that pushed him to that final edge of desperation, if he'd known the pain that his loss would cause he would have never ended his life.*

We ultimately found our way back to daylight with the help of our family, friends, and professional help. It is human instinct to survive. We don't forget or get over it, we just learn to live with it the best we can.

This kind of lacerating experience becomes part of our soul, embedded itself into our very psyche. Our unconscious keeps a permanent record of every

---

3 Carl David is also the author of *Bader Field: How My Family Survived Suicide* (Nightengale Press, 2008), ISBN #9781933449661.

moment of our life and reminds us of them vigorously when we try to erase or repress them. Having lived through and survived the horrific experience of my brother's suicide, I am awakened to the purpose of my life.

I am paying it forward by illustrating the pain with which the surviving family members are imbued so, perhaps, it will draw someone back from the edge of desperation. There are triggers that vault you backwards in an instant. When we hear of someone who has taken their life, our scab is ripped off and we weep with involuntary kinship. There is a common ground as we've been thrust into an unwanted membership to this God-awful club. We feel for them; we know their pain. We want to reach out to comfort them; to let them know they are not alone, they will survive; we all do.

It is always present, that persistent bit of pain which lurks just beneath the surface, waiting to nudge you back to reality when it awakens with just the slightest influence. We must acknowledge it and never shut it out, for we cannot deny who we are and all of the experiences that build upon our foundation. We take ourselves with us wherever we go.

As a father, my perspective had become even more profound. While our children were growing up, the haunts of the past were always there and our caution flags were always on guard. We never spoke of my brother's death until they were of significant age to understand and not freak out, as this is a very sensitive issue. We needed to let them know, almost as insurance, so that by understanding the degree of destruction such an act leaves on a family, they would never even consider it. This is my way of paying it forward, by taking the darkest days of my life and helping others...it is what we do with the information that makes us who we are in the end... I am on a mission to save lives...even one.

Trusting the Timing to God

On a November morning, as all the kids were getting ready for school, Lacey realized that Jack, 16 years old and her youngest—by a mere few minutes to his twin brother—was not up. She went into his bedroom and found him. He was hanging by his pink Ralph Lauren shirt surrounded by books about suicide. They were for a school paper. Jack left a note; it was identical to a suicide note that had been featured in Rolling Stone magazine [many years before]. He had been such a beautiful boy.

The November weather had been dreary. Jack had recently broken up with his girlfriend and his grades had dropped. It was just after Thanksgiving, and Jack was immersed in the topic of suicide for a school report.

Weeks earlier, Lacey had been watching a morning talk show that had a segment about suicide. When the twins came down for breakfast, she had said to them, "You wouldn't do this, would you?" And they both responded, "No way, Mom."

Lacey doesn't remember getting through the large funeral in her small village. She was in a daze; the entire community was in shock.

Jack's four siblings were doubled over in pain; they were furious that Jack took his life. Lacey was angry, too. She made the decision to focus on her four living kids. They were suffering mightily and she needed to be there for them. With determination, she put Jack on the back burner.

Prior to Jack's death, Lacey had watched a family friend, Mrs. Donahue, deal with the loss of her own son. Mrs. Donahue never let go of her grief. Swathed perpetually in black and drinking her grief nightly, Mrs. Donahue continually bemoaned the loss of her favorite son. In her drunken reverie, she would tell her remaining son that she wished he had died instead. Lacey was grateful to Mrs. Donahue; she learned some powerful lessons on how not to deal with the loss of a son. Lacey would focus on the living.

Lacey said it was her faith, as well as Mrs. Donahue's example, that made all the difference in her healing.

Lacey said that God told her, "When it comes to births and deaths, the time, the way, and the place are mine." She also felt that God gave her the faith to believe those words. Lacey views death as a sacred mystery.

Lacey inscribed the back of Jack's tombstone with, "God will heal us if we allow Him."

Social Media and the Teacher,
as told by Mohanalakshmi Rajakumar

Mohana, a 30-something university professor and writer, lost three people to suicide in 2011. She knew each person in a different capacity, but that did not mitigate the enormity of the loss and shock she felt. Each death—a gifted student, a friend, an acquaintance—was devastating in its own way.

From all outside appearances, the gifted student appeared to be a golden girl, but there were mental health issues. This student took her life on December 26; the timing was, needless to say, very bad.

Mohana's good friend's death by suicide was a shock; after being missing for several days, his body was found in his apartment. She realized then that you never really know what's going on with the people you love, even when you think you know them well. She was saddened by her friend's death, particularly because they hadn't seen each other in years, and the last time he had called, she hadn't recognized him; he sounded so different.

Then, yet another death, this time of an acquaintance, later that year, was the final bolt out of the blue.

Three deaths by suicide in one year were very sobering. They gave Mohana pause. She needed to do something and mobilized what came most naturally to her: she began a dialogue about dark feelings in an effort to educate people. Mohana posted the pictures of her friend and student on Facebook as memorials, as a way to remind people that suicide happens. She wanted people to talk without fear of judgment, and she used Facebook to continue the conversation. Mohana hopes that others will not feel so alone or desperate, and perhaps another tragedy can be prevented.

Kathy and The Compassionate Friends[4]

he Compassionate Friends is a self-help group with worldwide chapters for parents who have lost a child of any age. They also offer support to grieving grandparents and siblings. Illness, murder, addiction, suicide, manslaughter, drunk drivers, freak accidents, stillborn deaths—you name it— these folks have walked through that fire. It is unimaginably heartbreaking. And, yet, they gather and laugh and cry and help one another breathe again.

---

4 I had the opportunity to present at The Compassionate Friends International Conference in 2012. This essay is distilled from many of my conversations and interactions with the attendees, all of whom had lost a child, grandchild, or sibling, many by suicide.

Kathy told me that since the death of her son by suicide, she has lost all of her friends, and that is why she first went to The Compassionate Friends annual meeting. Other parents told me similar stories. It's not that the people in our circle of acquaintances are bad, they all said. They just don't know how to handle the weight of the grief. They don't know what to say, how to say it, or they nervously make inappropriate or inane comments.

For example, one father told me that as he walked out of his son's memorial service and settled into his car, his brother-in-law talked non-stop about his own son's current career concerns. The bereft dad looked at his unaware brother-in-law and responded, "At least you have a son."

The parents acknowledged that many of their friends and loved ones were uncomfortable talking about death. Others told me that they felt it was too much of a burden for many of their friends. These parents who have suffered loss have come to recognize the "squirm" in others who do not know how to respond. Yet, these parents who lost a child want to talk about their sons and daughters; they never tire of the subject, and the conversation keeps their lost loved ones alive in their hearts.

One week, at Kathy's local group in her hometown, five new people attended their first Compassionate Friends meeting. That week, each new attendee had lost a child to suicide. It was an emotionally intense meeting. Kathy said that she and another mom connected. In the weeks that followed, the new mom reached out to Kathy for support and guidance. Kathy said that was a turning point for her—in saying yes to the other mom-in-need, Kathy decided to live. In helping another mother, Kathy found her reason to keep going.

The Way of the Heart, by Antonia Nelson

I first experienced suicide in my family at age 18. My sisters and I were told that my uncle had died from an aneurysm. Years later, when someone asked about my uncle's suicide, I remembered that I had picked up the upstairs phone and over-heard the sheriff tell my father, "He would be bringing the guns into town." Guns?? The story had always been an aneurysm, never a suicide. Now it made all made sense to me.

My mother, who had been sexually abused as a child, tried many times to take her life with prescription medications. Her nurses said years later, after she had passed, had she received the kind of help she needed back then, she would not have been over-medicated her whole life.

Years later, my son's best friend, whom we had known since kindergarten, took his life. He was 18 years old. It was so hard for the whole community, and especially his friends, these young men, to have lost one of their closest friends.

I thought I was "okay." I tried to do everything I could to hold it together. I got some of the young men to a few sessions of group therapy and that was good—and it was not enough. About six months later, I moved and started a new job working at a Myofascial Release Treatment Center in Sedona, Arizona. I thought all was well until I began experiencing extreme body pain. The pain was growing day by day; I thought I would have to leave my job. Ironically, the clinic where I worked was for people who had experienced a trauma, injury, surgeries, etc. These people had exhausted everything in the medical model, had not healed, and were still in great pain. I prayed for something that was going to help people heal more permanently, and prayed for myself to heal and get out of pain.

Months later, a friend from Canada came down for a myofascial class, and she looked completely different. She shared the work she had been doing and said, "The teachers live right in Sedona, go check it out." I did, and during the last 15 minutes of a one-hour session of The Way of the Heart, I was asked, "Is there anything that continues to cause you stress, over and over?" Hmm…I had to think; nothing was coming up.

There was the grocery list of sexual abuse, rape, alcoholism, prescription drug abuse, and a slew of other things that no longer held any charge. And, then, the volcano of emotion came flying up—tears, sobbing, snot running. It was the suicide of my son's best friend. I couldn't talk; I couldn't breathe; all of it was racing through my brain. In about 15 minutes of working through the all the steps of the event with the facilitator, there was breath again. The tears stopped, and I was able to talk about it without dissolving into a puddle. The best part was that the 2,000 pound wooden yoke that had been strangling my neck and shoulders was now gone.

This feeling was all new. I wasn't quite sure what had happened, but I knew in my heart that I wanted to feel like this every day and to offer this work to clients. I asked the facilitator, "Where is the next class?" and signed up immediately. That was 15 years ago, and I continue this work every day, for myself and with my clients. It has been an awesome ride!

For 9 months, 3 days a week, I volunteered at Vets Place Central, a transitional housing center, in Milwaukee, Wisconsin, where I offered The Way of the Heart work. It was powerful to witness how The Way of the Heart helped resolve PTSD issues, all kinds of trauma, injuries, accidents, addictions, and more for the vets.

One of the vets I worked with took his life. He was so filled with guilt, remorse—so many self-limiting belief systems about himself that it made it hard for him to go on. My teacher shared, "He didn't take his life. The programs took his life." All those parts of himself that he thought were bad and wrong; he wanted to be whole and was not able to see the disowned parts. Through this experience, I have realized that "shadow work" is so important for permanent healing.

I have worked with a number of other clients who were contemplating suicide. One, I remember vividly. When he was 7 years old, his father took his own life. Years later, he, too, tried two or three times to take his life and was unsuccessful. He was coming for massage and was in a lot of pain. Something nudged me to share The Way of the Heart with him that day. In an hour, we were able to digest some of the trauma, and the healing began. A few weeks later, he called and shared with me that he had planned to take his life that day; thankfully he did not, he is alive and well, and a wonderful man and gifted artist.

This work is so powerful in helping people reclaim their lives, see who they truly are, and live the "why" they are here.

I Miss My Brother, by Barry A. Popkin[5]

$\mathcal{J}$ visited my brother Arthur every time I was in New York. After he came back from a year of serving in the military in Viet Nam, I never knew what I'd find when I visited him. Once I found him, my second oldest brother, with a needle of heroin sticking out of his arm. Another time, it was really terrible, I found him on his bedroom floor so stoned, and out cold, that he was actually turning kind of green and purple. I jumped down on the floor in a panic, and I started to give him mouth-to-mouth for about twenty minutes. All the time I

---

5 This is a condensed and edited version of the chapter, "The Hemlock Society," taken from Popkin's *The Death of God in New York City*, a family biography (ISBN# 978-1-4675-2411-7).

am thinking, *He actually killed himself this time*, when suddenly he gags and takes a huge breath while saying, "Man, am I stoned!"

Arthur's life got worse every year. His eccentricities as a kid started to become depressingly weird. It seemed that every minute of Arthur's existence was unbearable torment for him. Each second of breath was an excruciating pain. He woke up in the morning planning how he was going to kill himself.

The next two years went by, and they were filled with unbelievable attempts as Arthur tried to end his life. Some say suicide is cowardly because you don't have the human strength to face life. But, after a year, I thought he was amazingly brave. He'd get up every morning, saying to himself, "How am I going to try killing myself today?"

Once Arthur waited on a train platform, and right before the train comes, he jumps on the tracks. He left the station on a stretcher bruised from head to toe and totally blackened. Somehow, my brother survived.

A week goes by and Arthur leaves his apartment one night after taking twelve sleeping pills. He drives his car to a dark, secluded spot, attaches a hose to the back exhaust pipe, and puts the hose in the back window. Arthur closes all the windows and starts the engine as he begins to fade away. Minutes later, the cops pull up and immediately recognize the state he is in.

One week after that, Arthur is with his Italian friend, Nando, who worked nights in this pizza place. They are both sharing a heroin needle, both getting off. Nando went up front to take care of business. While Arthur, already stoned, wraps himself in a wet blanket and slips inside the big commercial oven with the gas on.

Nando smells something funny from the back room. He finds Arthur in the oven, cold and clammy. He appears to be dead. Nando and his uncle pull Arthur out of the commercial oven and carry him outside. They both think he is dead, but Arthur wakes up.

Shortly thereafter, Arthur is forced into a hospital for mentally disturbed people. They couldn't help Arthur in any way, even the electric shock treatment they gave him didn't help. Not only was Arthur deeply depressed, now he was mad as hell.

Soon he was out of there, I took him back to his apartment, and I noticed he was reading the Hemlock Society book. He was trying to find more exotic ways of killing himself.

I was concerned and tried to help him in many ways. I knew this guy's existence was pure agony. Something had to be done, but his despair was beyond help. I felt lost.

It was my desire to help Arthur, but his view was so infected with delusions, despair and torment. It was a miserable reality. I finally started to understand and see a different view of his life. I did not resist him and his talk anymore. I just listened as he explained to me, in detail, his second-by-second torments. I sort of understood and only had one more ploy to try and help him. We talked about the yesterdays—that's when I'd pick up a small grin on his face, remembering the times we'd had fun.

I said to him, "Listen, Arthur, if you are going to kill yourself, why don't you go out with a bang?"

What I meant by that was if killing himself was to come, and it seemed we could not stop him—he had tried again the day before—then he might as well have some fun, and buy himself a car so he could get out of his depressed, crummy, lonely apartment. Furthermore, why didn't he spend his money and try to enjoy himself? Then, if he wanted to go out, go out with a bang.

I made it my business for Arthur to have fun.

At least I proved it was possible for him to actually smile. I was happy seeing him smile and being in the moment instead of seeing his inner torment. But the happiest moment was when we got back to his shitty, lonely depressing place. I dropped him off exhausted, but he was in a tired, happy place. He looked at me and said, "That was really fun," and ran upstairs smiling.

But Arthur had finished reading the Hemlock Society book and was off to new tricks. I started to hear stories from two of his friends about some unbelievable attempts to end his life again.

Camping with his friends, Arthur walked out into the night. It was below freezing, probably about twenty degrees. He continued walking for about a half hour. He took off his jacket and hat, swallowed some pills, and tied his feet and body tight to a big tree. Then he took a chain and lock out of his bag. As instructed in the Hemlock Society book, Arthur swung the chain around the tree as he sat up tight against it. He pulled the chain hard up against his chest and locked the chain in its most secure position. Then, he threw away the key and waited for his fate. He was shivering wildly, but soon he stilled because of the pills. The light snow during the night made it easy to find Arthur. His friends managed to release him and got him help.

Days later, Arthur is back to his crummy apartment. You just can't kill this guy. Somehow if the body is not ready to die it just goes on. But he doesn't have to think how to kill himself today because he is pretty much almost dead with pneumonia.

This unbearably sad story goes on for about two years. One day a priest from Elmhurst Hospital in Queens calls me at work to tell me my brother Arthur is dead.

Arthur went to Queens College and graduated in the sciences. These days, he had been working for the city as a lab tech. Very early that morning, before anyone was at work, except one other person, I understand that he disappeared off the face of the planet. Because I could never find the other person to ask him questions on what he might have witnessed, all I know is that Arthur came in the lab and blew up the enclosure.

I miss my brother every day.

Imponderables

— for Jeanette or henry

Tuesday in homeopathy class
"imponderable" remedies

moonlight blue
sun

I want to take
luna 200c
to feel the waves more,
come and go with my grandmother

Thursday I hear
that you are gone

all smiles, good soul
you took yourself away

transparent you
transparent me

    where did the veil go?

laugh at us
as we try to understand

mercy, moonlight, madness

my heart, my heart, my heart

my feet wet in all this rain

    — Dianna Vagianos Armentrout

Chapter Seven

Shared wisdom

During my many interviews, I would often ask, "What advice would you give to someone who is now going through what you have gone through?" and "Tell me how you have coped and what you have learned." Not surprisingly, the responses had common themes. I deliberately left these words anonymous. In the sections entitled, "Survivor Wisdom and Advice" and "How Did you Cope?" you will read gems of counsel, advice, and wisdom, born from the first-hand experience of those who walked through this doorway of loss and grief. They understand all too well the impact of suicide on loved ones.

Survivor Wisdom and Advice

What advice or wisdom would you pass on to someone who has just lost a loved one to suicide or how has the suicide changed you?

~ "If I had to tell someone who is a survivor of a loved one who committed suicide, one piece of advice I would say is experience the wound; experience the shock, the trauma, and let it wash over you knowing it won't destroy you, and trust that in time, like all wounds, you heal, and feel peace that your loved one is no longer suffering."

~ "Take comfort in yourself. You have done everything you could do. It's not your fault."

~ "He didn't leave me. It was just too painful for him to stay."

~ "There is no easy way to grieve. There is no right or wrong. Take the time to grieve and don't blame yourself. Practice tough love—the only person that can feel better is me. Recovering from grief is my personal responsibility."

~ "Let your loved one off the hook. Be happy if they are out of their pain. Tell them it's OK; it's not a sin."

~ "You never forget the suicide . . . it makes you part of who you are."

~ "Don't be afraid to cry in public."

~ "Take control of your healing journey."

~ "I would not trade any of the grief and loneliness for having known my love. I'd rather know him and lose him than never to have known him at all."

~ "Honor and treasure the past."

~ "Be kind to yourself."

~ "Forget closure. Allow yourself to feel the grief as much as you need."

~ "I think the biggest thing I learned is that you will never get over it, but you will get through it. There are so many emotions to go through, and it will take plenty of time, but you will end up okay in the end. I love that you used the term 'died by suicide' instead of that awful word 'committed.' Suicide is so often chosen because of the internal pain one is feeling on a daily basis. It's not an act of selfishness; sometimes it's the only thing that looks like a way out of this craziness we call life."

~ "Don't own their pain."

~ "I was blindsided. Get real support. I loved him. He was my heart."

~ "Stay the course."

~ "Not every suicide is mourned. My father's death freed the whole family from fear of someone who was probably a psychopath."

~ "Asking for help is not a weakness."

~ "The suicide person is in a better place. You couldn't have stopped or fixed them."

~ "My father's suicide made me really look deeper at my life. After his death, I had a dream and my father told me to go back to school. I did, and it totally changed my life [for the better]."

~ "People believe they have more control over other people than they do. You've got to let them go."

~ "If they can't live in the world, they have the right."

~ "Sin is a blame thing."

~ "The ones committing suicide made the decision. They chose to end their life. We choose to live. We control our own life and happiness."

~ "People commit suicide to get out of the hell of life."

~ "Suicide doesn't really have nice answers."

~ "Something good has to come out of this."

~ "There is an all too common expectation from society that we 'move forward' with life leaving our sadness and child behind. A truly impossible expectation. We all too often suffer the loss of family and friends for the inpatient attitude that exists towards the bereaved."

~ "Life is for the living."

~ "Talk about your loved one."

~ "We all have to experience everything—the dark as well as the light—and not judge."

~ "Initially, I was angry and sad, but I had to get over it to live my life. It was not my responsibility. It was her choice for her life. I can't live someone's life for them."

~ "I lost the gentleness in my life."

~ "Sometimes, death is an act of grace."

~ "It's a process. Allow the hurt. Be open to getting higher information from meditation. It's a lesson to be learned from. It's hard not to feel the guilt, the survivor's guilt. I understand the total despair and loss of energy. My father's suicide was the most painful death I have ever gone through. There was physical pain. I felt punched in the solar plexus for six months."

~ "After dealing with multiple family suicides and my own suicidal thoughts, I realized that I have more power than I thought. I have the power to choose to live a full and happy life. I value life."

~ "Acknowledge, mourn, and move on. You can get sucked into other people's energies."

~ "Don't judge."

~ "There were times I wanted to die, but I didn't. I have things to do on this planet and I don't want to repeat these lessons so I am plugging along."

~ "Suicide can be the ultimate temper tantrum."

~ "Everyone is from a different place. Who really knows what is going on inside someone else's head?"

~ "Guilt is for the birds. Yea, yea, it's 'natural,' but, really, is it? I say no. There is more possibility here than guilt. It's a worn-out belief system."

~ "Suicide was the only way he could shut up the voices inside his head."

~ "Nothing ever dies; energy merely changes form."

~ "I hate it when you lose your child that your life is never to be the same again. Life can be different and it can [still] be wonderful."

~ "Allow yourself to 'wallow' for a while."

~ "Don't pretend you're not hurting."

~ "Don't blame yourself. You couldn't be with them 24/7."

~ "Every suicide has their own reason for wanting death more than life. It was their own reason and they owned it by their actions."

~ "You can eventually come to terms with the fact that any guilt you are feeling because you didn't see this coming is unrealistic guilt. Suicides are very good at hiding their worst thoughts and feelings."

~ "Live in love or live in fear."

~ "Accept it."

~ "I had to forgive."

~ "Moving on is ultimately a personal choice. It is not disrespectful to the deceased; it is what they want us to do."

~ "No one mentions the very real pressures from relatives that occur after a suicide. Since there are varying belief systems all over the place, one has to decide and let others make their own decision without trying to change or feel responsible for the others. . . . Family dynamics can make it exceptionally painful to put the suicide in perspective."

~ "Friends . . . they know the date. They know what I am likely feeling but no one wants to mention it or talk about it. That is rather puzzling to me."

~ "I've been coached that no feeling is valid for more than two minutes. I don't know a lot about this, but believe it is likely to be true."

~ "We don't know everything."

~ "He did the right thing. He couldn't regain his physical life [after a near-fatal brain injury]. He was frustrated and lonely; he had no future and was filled with desperation. He followed in the footsteps of our father."

~ "Live the life they would like for you. And love, always love."

Suicide and death can cripple you or strengthen you.
I choose to be empowered.

— Audrey Stringer

I think being sad is another way of loving.

— Little N (age 5)

Endurance is my middle name and it has become
a fond part of my existence. We all have it,
just varying degrees.

— Kay Lewis

I would like to add my definition of hell —
it's going through life without the answers.

— Deborah Chamberlain

Be at peace because they are at peace.

— Peter Spinogatti

How Did You Cope?

~ "I constantly needed to talk. It reinforced that it was real—my child was gone. Talking helped to get it out. All that pain was stuck way down deep inside of me. My best friend just listened and listened. She was a great. She helped get me through it."

~ "My psychiatrist told me, "You can't carry someone around in your pocket.""

~ "Maintain a routine. Keep a schedule. Exercise."

~ "By doing things, that way you're not feeling guilty."

~ "I wrote my feelings down; it was a way of putting them outside of me. Later, I would go back and look at the list to see what had changed in me over time."

~ "Someone suggested to me that I visualize my son and to 'see' our times together. 'See' the encounters you had together. Did you care about one another? If *yes*, that is still a possession for you to keep for the rest of your own life."

~ "My children kept me going."

~ "I grew up sheltered and protected—the immigrant's story. It doesn't mean you won't be exposed, no matter how protected you were. You don't get the tools to deal with what life throws your way. Therapy and a survivor group gave me the tools. In the survivor group, I found comfort that I wasn't alone and I learned that I didn't know how long I had prolonged my brother's life."

~ "I had to do something in his memory and decided I wanted to raise awareness. I didn't want to be quiet about it. Parents were quiet about it. I started a 501c3."

~ "I got two tattoos as a reminder. On my left foot, there is the word 'ONE' and on my right foot, it reads 'OTHER' as in one foot in front of the other."

~ "I took a course in Grief and Bereavement and learned a lot and found a helpful resource."

~ "I spoke to mediums. It gave me the strength to go on. I felt a connection with my son and that brought me some peace of mind."

~ "We have an enormous extended family and they helped (as did strangers). There were lots of people sleeping over, cleaning, cooking, dressing us . . . we couldn't function."

~ "My husband grounded and anchored me."

~ "I realized what happens with schizophrenia."

~ "When we lost my sister, we needed to turn it into a blessing. My family does the 'Out of the Darkness' walk and other charity events to raise awareness and to honor my sister."

~ "Get it out; you can't stay in the toxic place. Journal. Express yourself."

~ "I wrote a book."

~ "Walking, non-stop walking."

~ "Part of my peace, really a large part, was making sure he had a funeral (my mother did not want to give him one or bury him with the rest of my family), that we read from the Old Testament and read the Kaddish. My stepfather was Jewish and I wanted to get as close to a traditional service as possible. He mattered; he had been in my life longer than my biological father who died when I was young. . . . I miss him; I cared about him and I know I did what was right in honor of him, and that is what helped me find peace."

~ "M. Scott Peck's book, *A Road Less Traveled*, helped me get through my father's suicide."

~ "I got educated about depression."

"I got involved with…"

◆ American Foundation for Suicide Prevention, *www.afsp.org*

Funds research, education, and treatment programs aimed at the prevention of suicide. Raises funds for research and visibility about suicide through "Out of the Darkness" walks.

◆ Fountain House, *Fountainhouse.org*

NYC community-based, "Dedicated to the recovery of men and women with mental illness by providing opportunities for our members to live, work, and learn while contributing their talents through a community of mutual support…'"

◆ National Alliance on Mental Illness, *NAMI.org*

NAMI is the "nation's largest nonprofit, grassroots mental health education, advocacy, and support organization dedicated to mental illness."

◆ The Compassionate Friends, *thecompassionatefriends.org*

International organization for "Supporting a family after a child dies."

◆ The Samaritans, *www.samaritansusa.org*

Samaritans USA runs individual Samaritan centers in the United States, and the parent network has 400 centers in 38 countries. Samaritans Centers "provide volunteer-staffed hotlines, professional and volunteer-run public education programs, 'suicide survivor' support groups and many other crisis response, outreach, and advocacy activities and programs to the communities we serve."

*Even in darkness,
it is possible to create light.*

—Elie Wiesel

Chapter Eight

The bridge not crossed: Stories from the brink

The Opening Questions

*D*uring my interview process, I asked:

◆ Have you ever been suicidal? If so, what changed your mind and your course of action?

◆ Is suicide still an option?

◆ What has made a difference in your life and helped you step away from suicide?

And, of course, there were times when my questions were of no consequence, and the story just spilled out in its entirety.

In this chapter, you will read stories of those who seriously weighed (and acted) on the choice to take their life by their own hand. Suffering enormous pain, these individuals hovered on the brink—often repeatedly—and were able to step back from the edge. Their pain, anguish, and often out-of-kilter biochemistry found some relief through professional help, medication, intervention, relationships, expanded thinking, spirituality, and love. Their experiences are powerful and, hopefully, a source of comfort for others who are hanging by a mere fingernail on the slippery slope of despair and hopelessness.

A few of the contributors chose to remain anonymous for personal reasons. Others said, *"No more secrets, no more hiding, and no more shame,"* and asked that their real names be used. And so they are. You will see this indicated by the "as told by" or "by" lines with each story.

There is rawness and intimacy in discussing suicidal thoughts with another. These stories from the brink are so very powerful. I am deeply honored and humbled by the willingness of these special individuals to share their very personal stories.

You will read of hospitalization, misdiagnoses, decades until the proper medication was found, a family history of postpartum depression, sexual abuse, a broken heart, feeling overwhelmed, bullying, and spiraling negative thoughts. You will learn how they each stepped back from the brink.

The "Bridge Not Crossed" shares the life stories of seven hugely courageous individuals. Each story is a teaching tale, as well as a healing story, that offers hope, understanding, and possibility. The chapter closes with individual comments from those who have felt suicidal. Their assorted words offer more insight into the minds and hearts of our troubled loved ones.

The Stickiness of Love

Sara is a medical professional and writer. She has survived a horrific childhood of unspeakable trauma. The following is her response to my questions about the very real consideration of suicide:

Yes to that . . . a long time ago and yet not too long ago at all in some regards. It was a time of a 'perfect storm' of overwhelm, where intense revisiting of old horrors and flashbacks was exacerbated through the reliving of a historical pain through a physical vulnerability after surgical intervention, and an impossible double-bind situation that threatened the safety of every safety that I'd managed to laboriously build into my life.

I was, in every sense of the word, overwhelmed. Fatigue, pain, frustration, anxiety, fear, weakness, vulnerability, and panic escalated in a cycle where abuse of power and apathy constantly kicked any handhold I could desperately grasp on to.

What changed my mind—at first tentatively and somewhat reluctantly—was love. The love others extended to me; the hope they held for me when I could not see any hope anymore; the possible light at the end of a tunnel that I could not fathom the end of, but they saw. The deciding factor in keeping me alive was the one factor that I could not control: other people's care toward me; their belief that my life was worth living even when I could not see it; and that the lack of it would devastate them even if I wanted to believe it was better if no one cared.

It was that trust—in change, in possibility, in me—that made the difference. It was a handhold that apathy and callousness could not kick out from under me. I could remove myself from the world, but I could no longer try to pretend that it did not matter; or that it won't hurt others. And as much as I was hurting; much as I wanted the pain to end; much as I could not see a way out of what was becoming a never-ending misery—I could not hurt others. I would not hurt others.

And someplace, in that tedious, horrible place, I got traction.

Others holding hope for me held me till my body healed enough to give me some perspective and some energy to try and even look at possibilities. . . .

Others reinforcing their empathy toward me, and their belief that there was something more for me to live for, gave me time enough to be able to look back and see that I've survived another day, and another, and a week, a month, a year.

I could live.

I found that a bit of light, from the light others shone for me, remained inside. The hope returned—small, flickering, uncertain . . . but there. I still needed support, but maybe less intense—love stuck. Attachment mattered. Caring registered and grew and took root and took hold. I grew. Hope grew. Life mattered. My heart expanded to hold quantities of love I could not have believed possible.

I thrive now, because of love.

Love holds life. Babies who don't feel loved and cherished wither. They fail to thrive. They, in every essence of the word, disengage and stop living.

It may have a different face when one is older, but it is still love that holds us connected to the living: love of the world, love of others, love of what one can accomplish, love of creatures on this earth, love of family, love of those who find love in them to give when one is not too lovable.

I don't know that love is felt by all the same way—but if one is capable of feeling love (and I believe anyone who is not a psychopath can feel love, and that psychopaths probably don't commit suicide anyway . . . it is too 'other oriented' to make it 'worth it' to them)—there is a way to reconnect the soul, to safety-pin a bit of life-thread to what seems unlivable.

For me, it was not being able to fathom hurting others in my path to escape my own hurt. I could not, would not, become someone who hurt others. It was not much, as empathy goes, but it was enough at those very dark moments. And it was strong enough even as that bit of tether, because that tether was woven out of love. I could not feel love for myself (pity ain't love, exactly . . .), but I could not dismiss the love others had toward me. I could not devalue them by pretending that they were so incapable of making decisions about who to care about, that they shouldn't have loved me. I realized, even in a place of darkness, that I did care. Not about myself, maybe, but about others.

Oh, I fought that—I resented it—I preferred not to have that tangling my escape-from-pain plans. But it was there. Tenacious and sticky and present; it was real.

And the reality of love heals.

From Patient to Doctor

*A*nnie grew up in the 1940s. She never felt like an ordinary person or like someone who fit in with the others. She describes her younger self as a "cute, sexy, little thing who never had any problems meeting men."

Annie admits that she put her parents through hell with her repeated 'suicidal gestures' and acting-out behavior. She had a difficult relationship and rivalry with her mother; her father was distant and tried to keep the peace. Annie repeatedly asked her mother, "Why did you born me?" Annie's mother, a voracious reader of psychiatry and psychology, turned to her own psychiatrist for answers about how to handle her daughter.

Annie's first suicide attempt happened during her college years when her older G.I. boyfriend threatened his own suicide if she did not marry him. Annie didn't want to marry him, so she climbed up a local bridge and planned to jump. Annie was rescued, expelled from college, and placed in a state psychi-atric hospital.

Over the upcoming years, Annie would be hospitalized on four separate occasions for a total of 24 months due to her suicidality, which frequently cen-tered on relationship issues.

During one hospitalization, Annie met Hank and she became pregnant. Once both were discharged from the psych hospital, they married and moved to a small city where their son was born in June.

A year after her son's birth, Annie was seriously unhappy with herself and who she had become. She couldn't feel love, couldn't deal with the emotional stress of raising her son, and there were a few moments when her behavior toward her baby son bordered on the abusive. Annie knew she was not capable of parenting him. Annie re-entered the state psychiatric hospital in June. Annie's therapist at the hospital helped her decide she didn't want to be married anymore. When Hank visited Annie at the hospital one day in early August, Annie told him that their marriage was over. Days later, Hank hanged himself.

When Annie received the news of Hank's suicide, she became very nause-ated and could no longer eat. She lost a tremendous amount of weight. She kept seeing the image of Hank's face contorted with anger and rage. Annie was diagnosed as schizophrenic.

Annie's parents took care of her son after Hank's death. Upon hearing of the schizophrenic diagnosis, both Annie and her mother realized that Annie could never care for her son. Annie's son was adopted at 20 months. Annie says she has had no regrets because she knows her son was given a much bigger life.

When Annie was discharged from the hospital, she came home and stayed with her parents. One night, her parents went out for the evening. Annie ironed all of her clothes and packed a small suitcase. She remembers being very detached. That night, Annie took all of her mother's medications, including 20 Nembutal—a sedative-hypnotic once used for the short-term treatment of insomnia—and went to sleep. Her parents came home and assumed their daughter had gone to bed for the night. At 8 a.m. the next morning, Annie's 36-year-old married lover from the psychiatric hospital, through many forceful machinations and contortions of hospital rules, insisted and succeeded in call-ing Annie. The call alerted her parents. They found Annie unconscious. Annie *was shipped back to the state hospital where she was intubated, remaining unconscious for three days.*

Later, Annie clicked with a therapist in the hospital who helped her enormously. At the time, Annie's diagnosis was amended to borderline personality disorder (BPD).

Ultimately, Annie was discharged from the psychiatric hospital, followed up with the residential after-care, and worked as a waitress. Her path led her to working with a dentist, later completing training, and becoming a physician's assistant (PA). At the age of 34, Annie entered medical school, which was a Herculean task given her ADD and difficulty in reading books. It turned out that Annie's favorite rotation was psychiatry. Her patients trusted her, and Annie found that she could look at the whole person—both body and mind—through psychiatry.

Annie says that she has worked for decades to successfully heal herself. She believes that it was her soul's plan to have those experiences in the state psychiatric hospital. Even though Annie showed no psychotic symptoms, it was the early 1960s and Annie was put on the antipsychotic drug Thorazine. Annie says her body was smart; she developed a rash two weeks later and had to be taken off the medication. Annie hated the feeling of no control when on the medication. These experiences have made Annie exceptionally empathetic to her patients who cannot take or tolerate medications.

Annie walked through the fire. She was able to transform her earlier experiences into wisdom, understanding, and compassion. Annie is now a practicing psychiatrist.

Thankfully, I Didn't Die, by Cathryn Green

Cathryn is a spiritual leader within her community. Her life has been filled with many struggles, including recurring bouts of depression. Cathryn was able to turn herself around with a great deal of personal inner work, professional help, tenacity, and faith. She writes:

I attempted suicide on two occasions in my life. My state of mind was such that I convinced myself that the world would be a better place if I weren't in it, and that even my children would be better off without me. I felt I was suffocating and being sucked into a black hole of grief and despondency with no hope of resolving it. Looking back now, I see the power of my own thoughts . . . they could have killed me!

Thankfully I didn't die and I recovered my sanity with a lot of help but also a lot of self-exploration. It is definitely my spiritual understanding that has emerged from these explorations and now sustains me when the depression seeks me out. My knowing of the afterlife enables me to remember there is no escape as such and that problems are to be faced along with the realization that earthly "problems" are temporary, no matter how difficult they may seem when we are living through them.

It took me a long time to recover from the guilt and shame I felt for attempting to take my own life. It was only the realization that I was indeed ill and that if I had been in my "right mind" I would not have made the decision I did, but it was a long process to forgiving myself.

From the vantage point of now, 30+ years on, I have compassion for the young woman I was and for all the efforts I made then and since to grow in wisdom. I am thankful that my attempts were unsuccessful and I was given the chance to continue my life. I am left now with knowing that no matter what life brings, I can come through and still enjoy life. I appreciate the gift that life is and I have no regrets.

I Didn't Even Thank Him, by Walter G. Meyer[1]

When I was twelve, my family went to North Carolina on vacation. I went out for a walk on the beach to be alone and cry. I couldn't cry in the shower like I did at home—all of us were in the same little motel room. I decided to wade out in the water. What I found out after I returned to shore was that the stretch of beach was posted "no swimming—rip tides." So the waves just sort of cut my legs out from under me. I wasn't a very good swimmer, but even Michael Phelps couldn't have fought this current, and I was getting dragged out to sea. And the most amazing thing happened. I didn't panic. I just felt relief. Relief that this was a good way for it to end. I don't know that I'd ever have had

---

[1] This is an excerpt from Walter G. Meyer's forthcoming novel *Triple Play* and is based on an actual event from his childhood (as a result of bullying) that took place in New Jersey. Meyer is a well-known anti-bullying champion.

the guts to kill myself. But this solved that. It would just be a tragic accident, and strangely, I was completely fine with that.

Then this asshole lifeguard shows up. How the hell he got there so fast, I have no idea. And he throws me that plastic can thing on a rope and tells me to hold on tight. For a second I thought about not grabbing it. But in that split second I had to do the right thing—I couldn't imagine what he would tell my parents. Even though I'd be dead, I didn't want him to tell my parents I chose to die. So I grabbed it. He pulled me in. He gets me on shore and wants to take me to my parents. He asked how old I was. I was so tiny he thought I was like eight. I stood there shivering and told him I was twelve and old enough to be on my own, so they had gone out and wouldn't be back for hours—it wasn't true, but he didn't know that. So he just made sure I was okay—and I was—I hadn't started drowning or taken in water or anything. So I convinced him I could walk back to the motel. God, I hated that son-of-a-bitch. He ruined my great idea.

I didn't even thank him then, I was so angry—for years after that I thought back to that moment and what a dick he was to ruin my big chance to just let go of my shitty life.

It's Always an Option, as told by Kelly Meister

" I am a childhood sexual abuse survivor who has made seven suicide attempts over the years. All were genuine efforts to end my life—as opposed to what many think is merely 'attention-getting behavior.'"

Kelly's father started molesting her at the age of two. Kelly's first suicide attempt was a drug overdose at age 17. She could not find any good in her life and no longer wanted to live the horrors that were her reality. She said they make suicide look easy in the movies, but it's not. She came to, a day and half later.

Another attempt landed Kelly in the locked unit of her local psychiatric hospital, and this became a turning point in her life. Kelly felt safe for the first time ever. Her father and the others could not get to her. Kelly was able to try psychotherapy. She said it was like pulling back an onion, layer by layer. Kelly learned how to work the system so she could stay in the hospital a little bit longer and feel safe and protected.

While in the psych ward, Kelly talked with the other women. It turned out they had much in common. Many allowed that they also held close to their heart a one-last-chance, no-fail option to end their lives. Their fallback option was: If all else fails, figure out how to get a gun and shoot yourself in the head.

As if on cue, days later, a woman with an enormous bruised egg poking out of the middle of her forehead appeared on the ward. This egg was marked with an "X" of big, black stitches. This woman had attempted suicide by way of a gun to her head. Her efforts had failed. The other patients were flabbergasted that she survived and equally horrified by what would be her legacy. The ER docs had not called in a plastic surgeon; they had stitched her up crudely with thick black thread. Like Hester Prynne's Scarlet "A" as her badge of shame, this woman would forever wear this "X" as a scar on her forehead and be marked for life.

Over the years, Kelly has peeled back many layers and done intensive inner work, but she is still haunted by her father. There are seven or eight bad memories every day, coupled with regular night terrors. To lessen the PTSD (post-traumatic stress disorder) noise in her head, Kelly is on an antipsychotic medication. Her life has been tough. Suicide is always an option for Kelly. "I did not regret any attempt; my only regret is that it did not work out. . . . It's kind of a curse to keep on going. It is so painful and so awful to live with all that is not fixable."

Kelly says that pets and animals have been good medicine for her. (Her book, Crazy Critter Lady, explains how the animals have kept her alive.) She allows the past has taken a lifetime's toll.

"I have enormous sympathy for those who suffer this much pain in a lifetime."

It Took 48 Years to Find Joy, as told by Anjela J. Dale

It started in high school. She had experienced deep episodes of depression over the years—her sophomore year in college, one year after the birth of her first born, and severe postpartum depression a year after the birth of her second child. Barbara had been bipolar since her teen years, but no one knew that.

The first time Barbara heard the word "depression" in relation to herself was 1972 from her brother-in-law, a Harvard doctor. Antidepressants worked for short periods, but nothing seemed to help for any sustained amount of time.

In 1982, Barbara was put on a low, daily dose of antidepressants. Barbara cried, thinking she finally had something to ease her daily life, but her depression still came and went.

Life was also punctuated by Barbara's periodic and vitriolic explosions of anger, which, along with her depressive episodes, took their toll on her children and husband.

In 1990 at the age of 46, Barbara divorced. At the time, she was only taking Prozac for depression. (She now knows she never should have been taking that drug alone, because it fueled the mania of her undiagnosed bipolar disorder.) That year, Barbara blew through her divorce settlement. Uncontrolled spending is a common occurrence for people with bipolar disorders.

"I got myself into a place I couldn't escape from—the worst depression came," Barbara said. "I was so disgusted with who I was and what I had done that I went into a very bad place." This was the summer of 1991. Barbara's family, who lived across the country, was on suicide watch; they called repeatedly to check on her well-being.

Over the years Barbara had thought of suicide. She made a concerted effort to keep things away from herself that she might use to take action and kill herself. "I knew there were moments when I would have ended it all with a split-second decision if I had a gun."

On the night of July 31, 1991, Barbara decided she was ready to end her life. She was in her new, post-divorce condo with the shades pulled down, sitting in the dark. "What got through to me was my sister, Betty, who had studied with Jean Houston for many years. Betty said, 'Barbara can die, but her body doesn't have to.' That thread kept me here."

So Barbara hunkered down in the dim light, perusing an old dictionary for a new name. Given her childhood fondness for angels, an "A" name was a place to start. On July 31, Barbara would have died. Instead, on August 1, Anjela— with a "j" for joy—was born.

In January, Anjela joined Betty in attending Jean Houston's Mystery School, and Anjela continued going for the next 20 years. This is the community where Anjela came to life and to light.

In 1992, the consequences of her spending caught up with Anjela. She was facing bankruptcy. Anjela was still on Prozac and diagnosed with major depression. Her psychiatrist wanted to increase the Prozac, but it was too expensive for her. He opted for lithium, and Anjela's life radically changed.

It took 48 years for Anjela's bipolar, formerly called manic-depressive, disorder to be diagnosed. Her manic side tended to manifest as anger, and it was not recognized as mania until the efficacy of lithium helped level Anjela's emotional states. As it turned out, the lithium also decreased Anjela's compulsive shopping to a level that was more manageable.

Anjela experienced another major depression in 1996. During that time, she had an out-of-body experience (OBE). She was very conscious of three beings in her bed: her present self, her soul, and her brain; they were all having the equivalent of a heart attack. Her body and soul watched as her brain was in terrible crisis.

"It was one of the first times that I realized, "I can get through this. This will end. I don't have to end my life. This is a temporary crisis."

This depression was triggered by menopause. Anjela discovered she needed hormonal replacement therapy (HRT) because of the chemicals they provide the brain.

"For me, suicidal ideation is always linked to the chemistry. I was missing something vital that was needed for the balance of my brain."

Anjela found a new psychiatrist, an incredible diagnostician. He prescribed the perfect mix of medications that she needed. She now lives a normal life, with the help of small, daily doses of three psych medications. Anjela is an artist and the meds have in no way affected her creativity.

Anjela carries a puzzle piece in her wallet as a reminder. "If you commit suicide, you are a leaving a hole in another person's life puzzle that is very hard to heal. If you die naturally, you leave a hole in other people's lives that heals naturally. My untimely passing would adversely affect the lives I hold dear."

In conjunction with her optimum medication mix and the years at Jean Houston's Mystery School, Anjela has been enriched immeasurably by Landmark Education work and the work of Abraham-Hicks, "the last piece of the joy puzzle."

"How sweet life is, knowing I was almost not here. . . ."

Suicide to Joy: A Tale of Postpartum Depression, Three Mothers, and Three Birthdays, by Yael Daphna Saar

I failed where my mother succeeded.

Make that "failed" and "succeeded."

My mother had postpartum depression after I was born. It got worse after the birth of my brother. She was 29 when she took her own life. My brother was three, I was six.

But this is no sob story. After my mother killed herself, she went up to heaven and searched for the best stepmother ever. My second mother, Mati, came to my life when I was seven. I have always believed that my first mother, Mina, sent Mati over to take care of the family she left behind.

When I was 33, I almost followed in my birth mother's footsteps. I swallowed a whole lot of pills and woke up in the hospital. Yes, in the psychiatric ward. I believe that my birth mom had something to do with the fact that those pills didn't end my life.

What a story, right? If I saw this in a movie, I'm not sure I would have believed the storyline. It would seem too conveniently orchestrated to make a point.

But wait, there's more:

With a lot of therapy, medications, and learning, I got better. A few years passed and I felt well enough to have another child. I thought that I knew enough about postpartum depression and hoped I'd be fine. I carefully weaned off my meds under the supervision of my doctor, got pregnant, and was fine until my second child was almost one year old.

Then, there I was, 38 years old and suicidal. Again.

While I attribute my postpartum depression to a hefty dose of genetic predisposition, I know that the real triggers were sleep deprivation and guilt. Both of my children went through long periods of waking up (at least) every hour. The first kid was born early, had oral motor issues, couldn't nurse and could barely drink. I pumped breast milk for hours each day, and he was spitting up my milk. He wasn't growing and wasn't sleeping. My second son was born on time. He was nursing fine, was growing fine, but when he was teething he wasn't sleeping.

To compound that, in both depression episodes I had completely lost my own ability to sleep. Even when someone else was on kid duty, I would lie in bed, awake and miserable. Whenever I did fall asleep, I would wake up after 15 minutes or so covered in cold sweat. I was drowning in a special combination of emotional and physical pain, which was a cold, bitter burn. It raged from my skin to my bones to my soul, like acid. I would look at the baby that I was supposed to love, and all I could feel was anxiety and resentment. I would look at my husband, who was doing so much to help, and all I could feel was guilt and inferiority.

I was hijacked by postpartum depression. My PostPartumDemons made it all seem very logical:

I'm a terrible mother = my husband and baby deserve better = they will really be better off without me = I should kill myself.

Considering my family history, it's not surprising that this actually made twisted sense the first time. But I was spared, and I wasn't going to waste my second chance at life.

With my second child, my suicidal thoughts did not include pills. My visions centered on my green belt (the one I am wearing right now as I type this). One evening I actually wrapped it around my neck and longed to pull it tight, but I did not attempt to kill myself again.

This time I did know enough about postpartum depression and anxiety to recognize that the horrible thoughts were really me talking. There were moments in which I could tell the difference between my real self and my PPDemons. In one of those moments I spoke up. I asked for help.

On the day before my baby's first birthday, I nursed him for the last time, and my husband drove me to the psychiatrist's office. I was actually prepared to be hospitalized again, but my doctor didn't think that was necessary because my family had the capacity to get into suicide prevention mode: someone was going to be with me at all times. I went back on psychiatric medications for postpartum depression. After weeks of not being able to sleep, I slept for 14 hours straight.

The next morning, I awoke to the sound of my six-year-old singing, "Happy birthday to my little brother, happy birthday to you." It was the day before Thanksgiving. I resolved never to try to kill myself again.

I wish I could tell you that I never wanted to die ever again. It took weeks before the suicidal thoughts were completely gone. But every time I felt the call of the green belt, I remade this promise: I won't kill myself today.

My recovery had many components, of course, but I sincerely believe I wouldn't be here today had I not internalized the concept that there is a fundamental difference between having horrible thoughts and being a horrible person.

Sounds basic, right? Why is that so important? Because when we are in the grip of postpartum depression, we forget this basic distinction. We forget the huge difference between suicidal thoughts and a suicide attempt. It's about as big as the difference between thinking that another guy is attractive and cheating on your husband.

When you are suffering, the thought of permanently ending your suffering is bound to be attractive at times. Illness, exhaustion, guilt, and shame cause millions of mothers to imagine killing themselves. The thought is so common it could almost be considered normal—which means we should prepare for it. When we are not prepared for the possibility of suicidal thoughts, we mistakenly see them as evidence that we are already such horrible mothers that we really should get out of the way.

My goal is not to stop the suicidal thoughts and the guilt; that would be nice, but it's just not realistic. My goal is to disarm such thoughts before and if/when they show up. I call this permission-based healing. When I'm allowed to have all my thoughts, I can lay down my weapons and pick up the shield. I can step off the battlefield and into a self-kindness lab in which I can learn and experiment with the many ways humans can heal.

But I don't believe we can heal while we are fighting ourselves: healing simply can't happen on the battlefield.

My healing involved giving myself permission to feel all of my emotions and learning how to treat my scared-self with kindness. Over time, I developed enough trust in myself that the depression receded completely.

After I got better, I heeded the call of my life story: I became a postpartum depression advocate and peer-support provider. I founded an online forum in which mothers from around the world learn permission-based healing and inspire each other to practice self-kindness. We call it Mama's Comfort Camp. This space is free and open to all mothers, from moms of newborns to grand-

mothers and every age in between. You are warmly invited to join us: http://www.mamascomfortcamp.com/.

Thoughts and Comments on Feeling Suicidal by Those Who Have Been There

~ *"Anger plays a major role."*

~ *"It creeps people out, but I can take my own life if I want to."*

~ *"Seeing my friend's pain [around a family suicide] has had a profound effect. I no longer want to hurt anyone that way."*

~ *"I didn't want the pain; I just wanted to sleep."*

~ *"Suicide is my out. It's my safety. I have comfort in knowing I have that option."*

~ *"People hold onto the pain to stay connected."*

~ *"My shrink says: Watch it, honor it, but don't feed it. Sometimes it tries to take over."*

~ *"Who would care?"*

~ *"Every time I stopped drinking, I stopped being suicidal. When I jumped off the bridge, I was drunk."*

~ *"When I am alone [bad break-up], that's when I start thinking about driving my car off the road."*

There must be those
among whom we can sit down
and weep and still be counted
as warriors.

— Adrienne Rich

Chapter Nine

How do we make peace?

Let's Begin

We have reviewed the facts—the commonalities, risk factors, reasons, and the range—and, as a result, have come to a greater understanding of the nature of suicide.

We have explored suicide from a variety of perspectives: teenagers and suicide, the military and suicide, maternal suicide, addiction as a possible form of slow suicide, suicide as an end-of-life choice, and the lesson of suicide.

Our hearts opened as we read stories and experiences from those who considered suicide and either turned away from the brink or were rescued and lived to tell the tale. And we resonated with the stories from loved ones who have rebuilt their lives and pieced together their hearts following the loss of their loved one by suicide.

In this chapter, we take a more in-depth look at the survivor of suicidal loss. We ask the question: Is it possible to find peace from such a devastating loss? From my perspective, yes, it is possible. And the peace we create becomes our pathway to healing.

You, the Survivor

Suicide leaves an ever-rippling wake of churning thoughts and feelings that are hard to shake. Your life has been changed in a dramatic, forever kind of way. You have taken it personally. How could you not?

You have been left holding the bag of squirming emotions and memories. There is the taint and taboo, guilt and remorse, rage and despair, confusion and regret, and the shame or guilt that somehow—and in some possible way—you are responsible.

Could you have done something differently? If only you had said something else... if you had been there ... if they had just talked to you one more time, maybe it would have been different. Most likely, not.

By one degree of separation, you are now a survivor of suicide. As with other traumas like catastrophic injury, illness, war, and childhood sexual abuse, this places you in a high-risk category for depression, substance abuse, post-traumatic stress disorder (PTSD), and increased suicidality.

Suicide elicits many jumbled emotions. Emotions are not good or bad; they simply describe the way we feel. And our feelings can shift and change. The enormity of the human heart is such that we can feel a wide array of feelings at once. We are able to hold a multiplicity of feelings that may be similar, unrelated, or totally contradictory. As a survivor of a suicidal loss, you might be feeling several of these:

◆ Afraid

◆ Angry

◆ Ashamed

◆ Crazy

◆ Depressed

◆ Devastated

◆ Dissociated and out-of-body

◆ Furious

◆ Guilty

◆ Heartbroken

◆ Numb

◆ Relieved

◆ Sad

◆ Self-recriminating

◆ Suicidal

◆ Stuck in a loop of "what ifs"

More than likely, your life has been turned upside down. Perhaps, you actually witnessed the suicide of your loved one, or you found the body or the residual aftermath. Or your mind's eye gave you the all too detailed image of what transpired. Your whole being is in shock and suffering acute stress. Your psyche is rattled and you are trying to absorb the reality of what has transpired.

Suicide takes the concept of complicated grief and ratchets it up exponentially to a new high. Suicide takes you, the surviving loved one, hostage. For the survivor, suicide is a game changer. It is life altering; your world feels incredulous, unbelievable, and surreal. It can be the day when time stands still. It can be the day you stop taking a full breath. And, unfortunately, it can also be the day people avoid you, talk about you, or blame you.

With the deep loss of suicide, you are vibrating with shock, grief, and disbelief. You are in extreme distress and you retreat from the din of dailiness. It is going to be a challenge to refind yourself and reclaim your desire to fully live again after a loss by suicide.

The Thunderclap of Sudden Death[1]

Frequently, suicides are sudden deaths. And sudden death hits like an enormous, out-of-the-blue thunderclap to the heart. Your world stops. This can't be true.

And, then, your brain frantically engages. One minute the person is here; the next minute that familiar presence is gone. Like a flame extinguished, you are

---

[1] This is adapted from a 2009 essay of mine, "How do you make sense of a sudden death?" http://www.religionandspirituality.com/view/post/1245040851569/; http://www.selfgrowth.com/articles/How_do_you_make_sense_of_a_sudden_death.html/.

plunged into a darkness that is incomprehensible. You become wild-eyed with questions and uncertainties.

You try to make sense of it all; you retrace your steps. You race back in time to the very last connection you shared. You think of the "Goodnight, Honey" or the "Don't stay out too late" to a family member or the "Have a good weekend" to the co-worker on his way out the door. The everyday words, the daily connections, seem so trivial and unimportant given the enormity of the loss, but they matter. They are the connective tissue of life.

Your mind, like a search engine run amok, comes up with all the related memories and associations. You remember the shared laugh over a quick cup of coffee. You think of the sharp words about keeping the curfew or who is going to pick up the quart of milk or your need for a vacation day.

You remember yesterday, your last week, last year, the day they were born, the day you got married, the day they walked into your class, your job, your life. Whenever and whatever those points of intersection, the moments of laughter and love, the hard times, the good times, the better times, the hang-out times, you want to remember it all — in vivid, painstaking detail.

Images and words jump to the fore. Your knees buckle at the image of reading him a bedtime story or brushing her hair. Bath time, bedtime, play time, work time, lunchtime, sleep time, making love time, finishing the project time; it all spreads before you—a diagram of your life with that person.

You find yourself choked up; words, memories, and feelings are caught in your throat and chest. It is difficult to take a deep breath. Everything feels so fragile and precious now. It is hard to navigate these uncharted waters; you lurch from side to side, feeling broken into a million little pieces.

Sudden death leaves you shattered.

What If the Suicide Was Not So Surprising?

Years ago, I worked at an urban drug clinic. In my early days, I was assigned a new client—let's call her Mimi—for my caseload. She was being released from long-term care in a psychiatric hospital, where she had been hospitalized for a near-fatal suicide attempt. It was her seventh attempt; Mimi had lethally drugged her dog, and she had barely survived herself.

At our first meeting, Mimi said she wished she had succeeded in taking her life and could join her German shepherd. At our next two sessions, Mimi talked less about suicide and focused on the possibilities of work or school. At our last session, Mimi uncharacteristically bounced into the clinic. I had never seen her so happy. I was thrilled. We made an appointment for the following week, but that never happened. Mimi had secured another cache of drugs and ended her life at a local motel, hours after our session.

As a young therapist, I did not realize that Mimi's unusual happiness, given her psychiatric history and prior emotional states, was an indicator that she had decided to take her life again.

Individuals who have been in and out of psychiatric hospitals, have attempted suicide multiple times, and/or have dealt with the extremes of bipolar disorder are at high risk for suicide.

Their families and loved ones have lived through the duress of chronic crisis states and the cycles of hospitalization, new meds, and help. Suicide threats are far too common in their households. These families have witnessed the get-out-of-my-life locked doors and the crashing explosions of fury; they have listened to the refusals to be hospitalized or take meds. They have seen the mind of their mentally unstable loved one unravel with delusions, spiral with grand plans, and crash with tangled emotions and distorted thinking. It is exceedingly difficult, stressful, and heartbreaking for everyone.

And, if the unstable one ends his or her life, it is often not a total surprise. Suicide has been percolating on the back burner as a possibility for some time. It doesn't lessen the impact of suicide or the heaviness of grief. Sometimes, however, there is relief that their loved one is no longer in agony. Their loved one is now free from the internal torment and, hopefully, has found a place of peace.

Grief and Dealing with Loss[2]

Loss is universal. It is also idiosyncratic and unique. We each handle loss in our own way. There is no right or wrong way to come to terms with death.

---

[2] Parts of this are adapted from a 2008 essay of mine, "Grief: Yours, Mine, and Ours"; see http://www.religionandspirituality.com/view/post/1221639913379/Grief_Yours_mine_and_ours/.

It is hard, exhausting, and excruciating work to make sense of the un-sensible and to unpack and repack a life that you have held with such love and affection. You will need time and space to work through all the layers of feelings as you remember and revisit all that you experienced and shared with the one you lost.

Loss requires time, time to accept the unacceptable and time to feel the undulations and reverberations of your loss. There is no time limit—grief takes as long as it takes. Grief opens you up in ways you never thought possible. Unexpectedly, you will find yourself remembering other losses in your life as well. Grief builds upon grief; like pearls strung on a necklace, every loss becomes connected close to your heart.

Trauma is also a cumulative experience. We hold traumatic events in our cellular memories. They are not forgotten. And like grief, a new trauma can trigger feelings from a prior trauma. This is important to consider, as suicide is both a traumatic and grief-filled experience. The double whammy of grief and trauma can sometimes be so overwhelming that it is hard for you to stand or eat or sleep or even make simple conversation. Dealing with a suicidal loss requires extreme gentleness as you wade through the minefields of emotional residue.

Understand that grief can be crazy-making. Your world is upside down and nothing makes sense. You have lost the *terra firma* upon which you have grounded yourself. Now, everything is up in the air. There are no more givens or constants; everything seems like a variable. One ER nurse told a grieving mom, "Do not be surprised if you hear the voice of your daughter. It is not abnormal to hear voices of the deceased, especially at the beginning."

There is no one way to grieve and deal with loss. It is the difficult process of both accepting and letting go. It is also a process of finding peace.

Love is very much like courage,
perhaps it is courage, and even
perhaps only courage.

—Galway Kinnell

The Cycles of Life and Light

In the cycles of life, there is birth, death, and rebirth. This cycle is most evident in Mother Nature, but the same holds true for our human spirit. Every one of us has encountered setbacks, losses, and personal moments of devastation. In turn, we contract into ourselves. We make our lives smaller and more interior. We cut away the non-essentials. We feel hollow and empty. We crumple into a small space and desire solitude. For a time, this becomes our new normal. We find comfort and safety within our own small, tight, darkened corner. It is perfect for our survival.

This tight, dark space serves—perhaps unwittingly—as a gestational space, a personal chrysalis. We are held in a suspended state of non-ordinary time, floating in the subterranean depths of our heartache. It can be hard to see in the dark, but there is change afoot. The journey of grief is realigning us in ways we cannot name.

Musician Leonard Cohen told us, "There is a crack in everything, that's how the light gets in." And so it is with the devastation of deep grief.

There is some flash of insight, inspiration, acknowledgment, or truth—our version of light—that pierces the darkness and encourages us to expand beyond the tightness, grow beyond the smallness, and feel more of the light. We begin to emerge from our personal depths, in our own time and at our own pace, and embrace life more fully. However, we are no longer the same person. Death and loss have rearranged our cells. Grief has pounded our hearts and shaken our being. We have swum in the darkened depths and now we have resurfaced. We see with new eyes. We operate with a newly pieced-together heart.

Three requisites for change and healing

Suicide, like any major crisis, requires healing and a return to wholeness. It can also serve as a catalyst for transformation.

However, before there can be healing, there has to be a willingness to take the first steps toward change. Acceptance, forgiveness, and compassion are three elements necessary to facilitate change. They also serve as the building blocks to a foundation of peace. And, as we know, there is no healing without peace.

There is also no healing without feeling. Feeling is non-negotiable; you have to feel to heal. You cannot think your way to lasting peace. Your heart's attendance is required as you consider the doorways of acceptance, forgiveness, and compassion on your healing journey.

1. Acceptance

As with any healing, we start with acceptance. It's the first step and it requires that we cease and desist. There is no more battle, no more war within ourselves or with others. We put down our weapons. We no longer rail at the gods. We come to the place of acceptance, and this creates a space and a place for healing.

Acceptance opens the door to fresh air and new energy. What we have been battling, resisting, and fighting is no longer the focus of our energies. Our energy moves from battling the past to accepting and being open to the present. Acceptance provides a clean sweep so that we can deal with the reality of what is—even if we hate that reality.

Until we accept our reality, we cannot change. Acceptance is mandatory for healing and making peace.

2. Forgiveness

If we do not forgive, we stay stuck. We remain in the past. We stew in our own juices of rage, anger, bitterness, and hurt. Forgiveness has nothing to do with the right or wrong, good or bad of the other person's (or your) actions. Forgiveness is all about letting go of that which burdens *us*. Forgiveness allows *us* to release that which hardens and constricts our hearts. In other words, we do it for ourselves. Forgiveness can be difficult. It takes courage and strength to forgive. When we forgive, the ego steps aside and allows the heart to take the lead. Forgiveness is excellent and high-vibratory self-care.

Forgiveness paves the way for peace, and it also serves as a precursor to compassion.

3. Compassion

The etymology of the word *compassion* is Latin for "love together with"[3] or "suffer with."[4] Compassion speaks to our emotional connections with and caring for others. When we hear of others' hardships, misfortunes, crises, or disasters, compassion is the response of the heart that says, "I want to help. What can I do? How can I serve?"

---

3 Wikipedia, http://en.wikipedia.org/wiki/Compassion/.
4 www.compassion.org/.

Compassion elicits an empathetic response of active caring. The subtext of compassion is this: We are all connected; we are all one.

For those walking the healing path, compassion is the outgrowth of forgiveness and acceptance. When we have compassion, we walk in the other person's shoes. Our hearts expand and we come to understand and accept their (or our) actions and frailties.

Without acceptance, forgiveness, and compassion, our hearts remain shut down and closed. We are unable to move forward. We stay locked in a stranglehold of grief and heartbreak. These three steps are requisite for future healing and transformation, and they also serve as a pathway to peace.

It Always Starts with a Story

In earlier times, stories were always used as teaching tools. In today's world, we are surrounded by movies, television, and books. We binge on series. We love our stories. They are even making a comeback in the therapeutic world, where narrative therapy is coming to the fore again as a way to empower the individual to see the self as separate from one's problems and to acknowledge one's strengths and gifts.[5] And that is the beauty of stories: we get to see the fuller picture and understand ourselves in more mythic and archetypal ways.

And the truth is, from the beginning of time, we all love a good story.

This is my favorite healing story. I first heard this account in the early 1990s from higher consciousness teacher, Caroline Myss, who learned this firsthand from her friend and our protagonist, David Chethlahe Paladin. Lynda Paladin, David's wife, generously shared her thoughts and added immeasurably to the story.

I have shared this story[6] non-stop throughout the years. As I said, it's my favorite healing story. Like all stories that are told and retold, this story has morphed over time and repetition, and I give it to you like a well-tumbled stone that holds a mighty vibration.

---

5 http://www.goodtherapy.org/narrative_therapy.html/.

6 This 2008 piece was originally published under the title "Call Back your Spirit or Die" (http://www.shamanportal.org/article_details.php?id=797).

Without further ado, let's go back in time and let me introduce you to our hero:

David Chethlahe Paladin is a Navaho Indian living on a reservation in Arizona. David would laughingly say that his mother was a nun and his father was a priest. It turns out his mother became pregnant by a visiting priest. She, in turn, decides to become a nursing nun and leaves her son in the care of the extended family of their tribe.

David and his cousin spend a great deal of time leaving the reservation and going into town. They drink a lot, and they think life is better in the white man's world. The local constabulary is forever returning the boys to the reservation. By the time David is 13 years of age, he is an alcoholic.

David and his cousin determine that they are going to make it off the reservation once and for all—and they do. They find their way to California, wherein they lie about their ages and sign up for work with the Merchant Marines, where David befriends another young man from Germany. He also begins drawing; some of his sketches include the eventual bunkers that the Japanese are building on the atolls in the Pacific Ocean.

World War II is declared. The US Army tells David that since he lied about his age with the Merchant Marines, he has a choice. He can go to jail for a year or enlist in the army. David enlists. He is a teenager.

The army tells David as he is a Navaho, they are going to drop him behind enemy lines and use him as an information gatherer in their special services. David, using his native language, is to relay his findings to another Navaho in the army. Their language is a code that the Germans are unable to crack, much less decipher.

David is dropped behind enemy lines. Ultimately, he is captured and interrogated for information. The German officers find him useless and direct that he be sent to a death camp and executed as a spy.

Imagine, if you will, the scenes we all have invariably seen of the railroad station and the platform filled with lines of prisoners being pushed into boxcars for transport to the camps. Here is David. He is being pushed and shoved into a boxcar. There is a German soldier behind him saying "Schnell, schnell" (quick, quick). David stops, turns around and looks at the German soldier. It is his friend

from the merchant ship. The friend recognizes David and ushers him to a differ-
ent boxcar that will send David to Dachau.

In the barracks at Dachau, David sees an older man, a fellow prisoner, drop
something. David bends down to retrieve it. The guard, who has witnessed this
moment, asks David, "Are you the Christ?"

The guard then orders that David's feet be nailed to the floor and that
David stand there with his arms outstretched for three days, like Christ on the
cross. Every time David would falter and crumple, the guards would hoist him
up again. In the middle of the night, someone would sneak in and cram raw,
maggot-covered chicken innards into David's mouth.

When the Allies open up this camp, they find David a mere shell of a man,
weighing maybe 70 pounds, and speaking Russian.[7] They turn David over to
the Russians. David later speaks English and gives his name, rank, and serial
number to the Russians, who transfer him back to the US military.

David is sent to a VA hospital in Battle Creek, Michigan, where he spends
the next two years in a coma. At the end of two years, his legs are encased in
metal braces, similar to what polio patients used. David, a young man, maybe
not even 21 years of age, is to be sent to a VA home for the rest of his life.

David asks if he can visit his family on the reservation. The answer is, "Of
course." David literally drags himself onto the reservation. He meets with the
elders of his tribe. They ask to hear his whole story. David tells them every hor-
rible thing that he endured. He is full of anger, rage, and hate.

The elders confer and tell David to meet them tomorrow at a designated
point on the Little Colorado River. David agrees and at the appointed hour he
arrives. One of the elders tethers a rope around his waist; others remove the
braces from his legs. They hoist David up into the air, and as they throw him into
the raging current of the Little Colorado River, they say, "Chethlahe, call back
your spirit or die. Call back your spirit or die."

David would later say that those moments in the Little Colorado River were
the very hardest of his life. He had to fight himself for himself. And he was able

---

7 Remember David sketching during his tour of the Pacific and speaking Russian when the
Allies first found him half-dead at the camp? It turns out that David was channeling the Russian
artist Wassily Kandinsky. In fact, Kandinsky's best friend came for a visit to the U.S. from Russia.
The friend, the story goes, told the press that after a long visit with David, he felt that he had
spent the day with Kandinsky.

to see the big picture; he understood why things unfolded as they did. For example, he realized that the raw chicken parts were meant as a source of protein to sustain him so that he might live.

David Paladin was thrown into the river as a very broken—and broken on every level—man. And David emerged out of the Little Colorado River like the phoenix out of the ashes. He had metaphorically walked through the fire, or, in this case, swum through the currents, and had come out alive. He was born again.

David no longer needed his braces; he became a shaman, teacher, and artist and went on to work with priests and addicts. He died in his middle years in the mid-1980s.

The reason this is my favorite healing story is twofold. It tells us how to heal, and it is applicable to each and every one of us.

Healing is calling home our splintered energies; it is calling home our disenfranchised pieces and parts—those parts of us we would rather ignore and keep hidden under the rug—in order to be complete again. We bring in those parts of ourselves that have been ostracized and deemed shameful, bad, or unworthy. In turn, we accept, we forgive, and we have compassion for our very human selves. We cannot heal—and become whole—if we do not claim the disowned parts of ourselves.

Healing is also letting go of the toxic and the outdated. This requires acceptance and forgiveness on our part. It is hard to let go and release that which is familiar, habitual, and even dysfunctional. Clearly, it has served us in many ways. It takes consciousness to discern and acknowledge that which no longer works. It takes courage and fortitude to release what we have held so close and to realize that it no longer serves our best interests. Like the pruning of a tree, we cut back our dead weight for future growth.

Ultimately, healing is an act of reclamation born out of love and compassion. We reclaim ourselves and, in doing so, we honor and accept who we are in all of our humanness.

Seven Steps to Make Peace with Suicide

Peace is an active state. It requires a conscious choice and deliberate action. With this in mind, I offer you this seven-step method to assist you in finding your way out of the rabbit-hole of devastation. May it help you to return to firmer footing, both emotionally and mentally. May it help you to make peace with your loss by suicide.

1. Tell your story.

Remember, it always starts with a story. And so it is with you.

Allow yourself to sink into quiet. Settle down and prepare to dive deeply into the story of what has been. Grieving a loss by suicide is unique to each individual. It can be tangled, messy, with many ups and downs; a sudden, searing loss; or something altogether different. Suicide is complicated and, most likely, so is the story of your connection and relationship with your lost loved one.

This first step is all about you telling your story—the good, the not-so-good, the bad, and the scary. No holds barred. Your task is to tell your story in its entirety. There is no right or wrong way to do this: simply speak your truth. You will need to reach into the crevices of your memory and piece together the unfolding of two lives intertwined.

In doing this, you give yourself permission to air out what has been stuck or static within you. You create inner movement as you access your thoughts and feelings. Like a mosaic under water, you allow all the bits to surface as they create a whole picture of the relationship you shared with your lost loved one.

To help get you started, here are some questions. These are not *the* questions, but merely suggestions to jump-start the process. You can start your story anywhere, you can go backward, forward, and sideways—any way that works for you. The only rule is that you tell your whole story.

What was the nature of your relationship?

Examples: *He was my son, always a colicky baby, and as he got older we noticed [...]. The first time I saw my wife, I felt [...]. My sister was always secretive [...]. We never thought there was a problem with our father; he always treated us like [...].*

What transpired over time?

Examples: *In high school, there was [...]. After the birth of his daughter [...]. Over the years, our relationship [...]. She counted on me to [...]. The teachers noticed [...]. I took him to a doctor who said [...]. The first time she went into rehab, they told me [...]. When he came home from Afghanistan, I heard him [...].*

What was your relationship like?

Examples: *He made me crazy with his [...]. I ignored [...]. We kicked her out of the house [...]. I fired him because [...]. I didn't know him that well, but my brother [...]. His friend said I was [...]. I refused to believe what she said about my husband [...]. I babied him until he was [...].*

What did the suicide do to you? What did you think? How did you feel?

Examples: *I went crazy for about two years [...]. I was furious; how could he do this to me? [...] Thank God, he's gone; I don't have to watch over him every minute of the day. [...] She was never a 100% after [...]. I tried to kill myself, but the gum jammed [...].*

Are you changed in any way?

Examples: *I am hypervigilant with my other son [...]. I don't wait any more, I call for help [...]. I am more accepting [...]. I am shut down [...]. I saw what the suicide did to the family, I won't take my life now [...]. I still cry every day...].*

Has the relationship with your lost loved one continued in any way?

Examples: *I play his favorite music and feel like he's near [...]. I dream of her [...]. I can hear my husband talking through our son [...]. I work on a hot-line and feel like my daughter is my guardian angel [...]. Our dog is always barking at one corner of the house and I think it's my son telling us he's around [...].*

Ideally, tell your story aloud. Share it with another trusted person who will bear witness. The other person is not to respond or question in any way. Their role is simply to listen and witness until you are complete. This is a powerful experience of honoring and acknowledging your journey. Make this a sacred moment. Light a candle or have a flower. Put yourself in an openhearted, mindful place, and allow the story to unfold and flow. It may shift and morph of its own accord.

Consider sharing your story three times (with three different individuals). Often, you will find that your storytelling prompts other memories, connections, and insights. Further, you might see with new eyes after the first round of storytelling.

Alternatively, you can tell your story to yourself. If possible, record your story and later listen to your words. Or you can write your story, read it aloud, and, perhaps, burn the pages when you have completed your ritual.

There are many variations on a theme. The essential part is to tell your story about the life you shared and the death you grieve of the loved one you lost to suicide. If you have a witness, it can make the experience more reverent, considered, and potent.

Trust your good instincts, honor yourself, and tell your story in a way that works for you.

2. Own your part.

No doubt, you are familiar with the expression "Know thyself." It comes from the ancient wisdom teachings, as do other teachings about being responsible and accountable for our actions and choices. This is the intention of this second step: What do you need to do take responsibility for your part in your relationship with your loved one lost by suicide? This requires self-insight and a willingness to take responsibility for your choices and to be accountable for your part in the relationship.

A. Reality Test
Allow yourself to get very clear about the reality of the situation with your lost loved one. What was the true nature of your relationship? Were you in any way responsible for the suicide? Realistically, could you have changed the outcome?

B. Forgive Yourself
We need to forgive ourselves for being human. We fumble and make mistakes. We all do the best we can with the consciousness we have at the time. We have moments where we react poorly, lash out in anger, or are stingy of heart. We can do regrettable things and then hate ourselves in the morning. The key is to acknowledge our missteps and forgive ourselves—and, hopefully, learn from our mistakes.

Where do you need to forgive yourself?

◆ Is it thoughts, actions, or words directed toward your lost loved one?

◆ Is there anything weighing you down about your part, presence, or absence in your loved one's suicide?

◆ Do you feel guilty for drawing boundaries to protect yourself or shutting the door on chronic addiction?

◆ Did you lose patience?

◆ Did you misread the signs?

◆ Are you ashamed and embarrassed by your loved one's suicide?

◆ Are you relieved that this time the suicidal action was fatal?

It is through forgiveness that we find relief from our heavy burdens of self-recriminations and judgment. When we forgive, we make peace with the past.

If you can't forgive yourself or others, can you determine why you resist forgiveness? What keeps you in this locked-down and hurting place? Do you feel you need or deserve to be punished? Do you feel righteous and justified? Are you holding onto an old belief system? What blocks your freedom to forgive? Do you believe your loved one would want you to suffer in anguish?

C. Forgive your Loved One

Anger is a frequent response to suicide. *Why did you leave me? Why didn't you tell me? Why did you do this to me?* The anger says, "What about me. What about us? We were connected in some way. We had history." Yet, no matter how much you loved and cared and pretzeled yourself in 1001 ways to help, it was not enough to keep your loved one alive. You are furious. And beneath the anger, there is a vast well of pain and hurt.

Even before the suicide, there may have been an upside-down life and a long runway of problems, disasters, and crises. There can be a great deal of anger, hurt, and confusion about what has transpired. Are you able and willing to forgive your loved one for his/her past actions and prior chaos? Can you forgive your loved one for that ultimate choice?

What would it cost you to forgive and let go?

D. Forgive Others

Sometimes, doctors, therapists, spouses, parents, siblings, children, friends, co-workers, and the like are seen as part of the problem—and not the solution. There can be anger directed at schools, churches, governments, VA offices, hospitals, and other institutions in which we (mis)placed our trust. There can be a need to blame an institution for creating the situation that leads to suicide. We might need a target for our anger and a scapegoat for our loss.

As we know, holding on to outrage and anger hurts us, not the one who is the object of our ire. Is it possible to forgive the professionals or the institutions for their role in your loved one's life?

E. How to Forgive

There are many ways to initiate the process of forgiveness. You can write a letter, talk to the grave, go to confession, do a ritual, work through it in therapy, make amends, do intensive journal work, complete a life review, and so forth. You can ask for forgiveness for any real or perceived hurts and harms that you caused, and you can offer your forgiveness for any real or perceived you received.

Clearly, there is no one way to forgive, but there are some common elements in the process: willingness, acceptance, an open heart, understanding that forgiveness is a personal act of self-care, and conscious and deliberate release of what was.

Forgiveness is predicated on acceptance—not agreement or approval—of the offensive action. It requires a conscious willingness to release the burden and toxicity of hurt, pain, and anger. Forgiveness lets go of the past and makes room for the future. Forgiveness is a shift of the heart from closed to open as well as a potent form of healing.

F. Bless and Release

You take the sting of hurt or betrayal and neutralize it with your forgiveness. Bless what you are ready to forgive and release. There can be gratitude for deeper lessons learned, understandings gleaned, and the clearing of your formerly entrenched and paralyzed energies. In other words, let go with a light heart.

3. Debrief the dark moments.

Suicide is often a crisis situation. When we have been through a crisis, we need to debrief. We need to give voice to our experiences. We need to put light on the unthinkable. It helps with the healing and decreases the trauma response to name the critical experiences.

A. What were the dark, darker, and darkest parts of the suicide for you?
When you lost your loved one to suicide, there were moments—before the suicide, during the suicide, or after the suicide—that left a lasting impression on your psyche or your mind's eye. There can be images, thoughts, sounds, smells, or feelings that you cannot shake. They loudly reverberate and repeat themselves within your being. These are personal moments; they could have even happened days or weeks before the actual suicide. Time is of little consequence in this context. What is important is that you identify your moments of darkness around the entire suicide and post-suicide of your loved one.

B. What were the worst parts?
For *you*, what were the worst parts of the suicide? What impacted you the most? How did you feel? What made you want to scream or run away? Did you want to die? What happened when you told family? How did you get through the funeral or memorial? What did you find when you cleared out a closet, a desk drawer, or under a bed? What were those moments and events that caused you further pain and distress? What made you feel the most vulnerable or ashamed or frightened or furious? Are you able to unpack your feelings?

C. What did you do well?
Conversely, as we look at the dark, we certainly want to include the light. It serves a purpose as well. It reminds us that we have strengths and wherewithal that we can draw upon to help us walk through this trauma and heartache.

What did you do right? Can you recognize where your unique strengths and abilities made the situation better? Did you surprise yourself with how you handled some of the details, relatives, or friends? Did you allow others to help you? Where are you proud of yourself?

Debriefing is a process of personal investigation. You pull out and examine all of the emotional details. As we discussed, we have to feel to heal, and this process moves us forward in our recovery work from deep suicidal grief.

4. Call back your spirit.

Previously in this chapter, you read my favorite healing story, "Call Back Your Spirit or Die." We are using the powerful message of this story as our template for the fourth step in our process to make peace with suicide.

David Chethlahe Paladin's journey teaches us that when we hold onto the negative and painful parts of our past, we remain stuck in our own unhappiness and frustration. As the Elders instructed Chethlahe, we need to call back our spirit or we remain languishing in a constricted existence. We humans tend to hold on; we struggle with change and conflict. Sometimes, we just "go along to get along." It seems easier; but over time, the incremental wear and tear of not being true to ourselves takes its toll. We end up feeling emotionally half-dead, unfulfilled and thwarted, and weighted with unresolved, unsatisfactory relationships.

Relationships are everything, and the way we handle and manage ourselves in all of our relationships is essential to our happiness and well-being. Chethlahe's story asks us to belly up to the bar, so to speak, and reclaim our life force. We are asked to be mindful and aware of how we act, react, respond, and engage with one another. We are called to take ownership of our lives. We are called to be our own best authority in how we expend our energies and interact with one another. We are asked to be coherent, true to ourselves.

A. Your assignment:
Hold the memory of your lost loved one in your mind's eye. Examine it through Chethlahe's eyes. Where did you lose yourself? What held you hostage? Were you compromised, victimized, or bullied in any way? Are your feelings about your loved one scattered in many different directions? What is unresolved? Are you carrying burdens of the dead that do not belong to you?

Consider what you might need to do to "clean up your side of the street"? How might you need to change to have more direct, honest, loving (toward yourself and others) relationships? Do you a notice a self-defeating pattern of behavior? Do you see where fear has blocked and inhibited you? Do you accept that you have a place at the table and you are worthy?

Consider these questions and any others that present themselves to you. Your goal is to feel that your relationship with your lost loved one is now clean. There are no more energy-sucking entanglements. You are able to bless and release the dead—the dead thoughts, old emotions, past worries, old patterns, and the like.

B. And, if you are so inclined, here are your extra-credit questions for your consideration:

◆ How do you choose to begin to live your life in resonance and authenticity?

◆ How will you honor your loved one going forward in a life-giving way?

◆ How will you honor yourself going forward in a life-giving way?

Calling back our spirit, our life force, is not easy. It takes time and practice. And we will need to do this repeatedly throughout our lives as we find ourselves embroiled in new situations and faced with new challenges. However, when we do call back our spirit, we re-empower ourselves and stand in our fullness. We are total-ly plugged into our mind, body, and spirit. And, from this place, we can make peace with ourselves and open the door to healing. Calling back our spirit is, indeed, good medicine.

5. What are the lessons?

There is no right or wrong to this question. This is a matter of reflection and person-al choice. You may feel there are no lessons—and, that's fine. It's all a matter of indi-vidual perspective.

Plato said, "The unexamined life is not worth living." I totally concur. From my perspective, there are always lessons to be learned from every experience. I learn about myself and others. How did I behave? What punched my buttons? Where did I hide? Why did I open my mouth? What could I have done better? Where was I graceless, tactless, or heavy-handed? What stopped me from fully showing up?

We learn how to be in the world, with ourselves, and with others through relationships. How we interact, feel, and think, both overtly and covertly, can serve as windows of self-discovery.

I also learn from looking at life through the big viewfinder and seeing the bigger picture. I find it helpful to have a take-away insight from my experiences, especially the tougher ones. It makes the harder experiences more meaningful, especially when I can see it as part of a larger whole.

If you are open to the idea of lessons to be learned, here are more queries for you to ponder that can serve as a starting point:

◆ What do you understand now about you, your lost loved one, and your life that you didn't comprehend before?

◆ Has your perspective changed since the suicide? If so, what do you perceive differently? Do you see life differently?

◆ How has your heart been changed? In what ways do you feel differently?

6. Connect with your loved one.

Through the power of love in our hearts, we are always able to connect with our lost loved ones. We carry the gift of memory; it is encoded in our senses. Maybe we hear a favorite song on the radio, catch a whiff of her perfume or his after-shave in the market, see something we once shared, or feel your loved one's hand on your shoulder. The sense of smell is particularly evocative. It is no wonder that we inhale her sweater or wear his shirt. Sense-memory is a powerful reminder of what we once shared.

For some, connection is also possible through signs and symbols. Often, these signs and symbols come through nature. For example, you see a rainbow or a hawk or a dolphin or a particular flower on the anniversary of your loved one's death and you know, without a doubt, it is message meant for you. If you are open to this concept, your world can become animated with signs and symbols.

Meditation A
In this step, you are asked to get quiet and connect with your deceased loved one. Give yourself about 20 to 30 minutes and allow this to unfold.

- Get in a meditative space: quiet, private, and peaceful. Make sure your spine is straight, and your arms and legs are uncrossed. You may close your eyes or keep them soft.

- Put your left hand on your heart.

- Focus on the midpoint of the sternum (the breast bone), and breathe in and out of your heart.

- Breathe love to your lost loved one. Put a half-smile on your face so that you are energetically open.

- Don't try to do anything; drop any expectations. Be present in a loving way.

- Direct love and light to your loved one.

When you feel complete, remove your hand from your heart. Wiggle your fingers and toes and allow yourself to gently come back into the room. You may want to stretch as well.

Meditation B

Once you feel comfortable with Meditation A, you may expand the experience with Meditation B, if it resonates with you.

- Get in a meditative space: quiet, private, and peaceful. Make sure your spine is straight, and your arms and legs are uncrossed. You may close your eyes or keep them soft.

- Put your left hand on your heart.

- Focus on the midpoint of the sternum (the breast bone) and breathe in and out of your heart.

- Breathe love to your lost loved one. Put a half-smile on your face so that you are energetically open.

- Don't try to do anything; drop any expectations. Be present in a loving way.

- Direct love and light to your loved one.

- Connect with your Higher Self. (Your Higher Self is the part of you that operates from a place of unconditional love and acceptance.)

- Imagine a pool of golden light. See, sense, feel, or know two chairs or sofas facing one another in this space filled with golden light. (Note: Go easily with yourself. If nothing comes readily to mind, simply make it up. You will be pulling from your psyche.)

- Call in the Higher Self of your deceased loved one and invite him or her to join you in connection and, possibly, conversation.

- When it feels complete, express your gratitude and thanks.

- When you feel complete, remove your hand from your heart. Wiggle your fingers and toes and allow yourself to gently come back into the room. You may be inspired to journal about your experience.

Whether through memories of a shared lifetime, sense-memories, or meditation, connection is always possible. And, for me, there is great comfort in that thought.

7. Make a commitment to peace.

Having worked through the previous six steps, you have done all the emotional heavy lifting. Brava! Now, it is time to concretize your inner work. What do I mean by that?

Think of this: We celebrate special occasions and memorable events in our lives. We exchange gifts, take photos, give parties, make a donation, send flowers, buy a ring, get a tattoo, knit booties, wave a sign, light a candle, compose a song, and all sorts of other wonderful, creative expressions to physically and visibly honor and commemorate an important occasion or special event in our life or the lives of our loved ones. May I suggest that you do the same with the completion of your process of making peace with the suicide? Is this not a hugely important healing step on your life path?

Healing has enormous ripple effects. In Native American tradition, there is a saying: *When we heal, we also heal seven generations forward and seven generations backward.* I like this idea. Further, whenever one of us heals, we also impact those with whom we share our lives. Healing of the individual can lead to healing of the group, family, community, etc.

With this in mind, here are the two strategies to complete your process. These actions take your peace-making and drop it down into the body, where you claim it, honor it, and give it feet so that you maintain your balance and equilibrium.

Assignment A: Write a Commitment to Peace

With forethought and following much soul-searching and inner work, you make a commitment to yourself. This promise is written and named a Commitment to Peace in which you pledge to yourself that you are placing personal peace as the intention of your heart.

This Commitment to Peace is akin to making a vow or a sacred promise to yourself. You sit down with intention and put words on paper (or the screen). These words are your assurance to yourself that you will endeavor to maintain peace around the suicide loss of your loved one—and perhaps in other areas of your life as well. This does not need to be long and windy; it matters only that it comes from the heart and speaks your truth. This is your commitment to you. You are choosing peace over chaos and internal war. The process makes your focus, intention, and commitment tangible.

As life is ever dynamic and we continue to evolve and unfold, you can always update and upgrade your Commitment to Peace as frequently you as you want.

Assignment B: Create, find, or fashion a symbol to represent your new place of being

In this context, a symbol is the 3D representation of what has transpired for you as you have deeply examined your life and your relationship with the loved one you lost to suicide. Your symbol will serve to remind you of the history you shared, the memories banked, and the love that continues. It will acknowledge and honor the path you have walked, the work you have completed, and the losses you have grieved.

Symbols are visual cues that can anchor us when the world gets stormy. They are physical reminders of what was and what is now. Your symbol will represent your connection with your loved one, your process, and your personal commitment.

Allow your heart to guide you. Sometimes, your symbol will show itself to you. You will know this is the one for you. Or you may need to create and construct a symbol that holds all of the layers of the past, the path, and the process. Needless to say, there is no one way or right way. Trust yourself.

In Closing

Please know that if there is any unfinished business or if something new presents itself, you can always return to any of the prior steps as needed. This is a process—a process of the heart—and not a straight line. Trust your inner voice and do the steps in way that works best for you.

With these seven steps, you have told your story, taken responsibility and practiced forgiveness, debriefed the darkness and acknowledged the light, called back your spirit, looked for lessons and the take-away insight, connected with your loved one, and committed to peace. This has been dense, deep, and intense work. You are to be congratulated for your fortitude as well as your willingness to take your loved one's suicide and transform the loss into healing.

The loved one you lost to death by suicide will never be forgotten. That person will always hold a permanent place in your heart. Hopefully, by way of this process, your heart has been widened even more in order to hold it all—the history, the heartbreak, and the suicide—with peace. May it be so.

A Note about Being Suicidal and Making Peace

If you are suicidal, have been suicidal, or are in a dark funk, how do you make peace with yourself?

You can use the seven-step process and focus solely on yourself. You omit all the parts referencing a lost loved one, and you direct all of your attention and energy to exploring the entirety of your emotional terrain.

For your process, consider what individuals or elements have had large emotional pulls on your well-being. Look at your relationships (with people, institutions, and substances) and discern where you have been influenced, co-opted, taken emotionally hostage, and the like. Your relationship with yourself as well as others is key in helping you to discover what draws out your darkest parts. Equally, your relationships will also show where you have been your best, performed well, and made yourself proud.

This model is designed so that you can see yourself clearly and, if you are ready, make changes and a commitment for a more balanced, congruent, and happier existence. May these seven steps serve you well.

Tibetan Buddhist Prayer

May you be at peace,
May your heart remain open.
May you awaken to the light
Of your own nature.
May you be healed,
May you be a source of
Healing for all beings.

Chapter Ten

Suicide and the soul: An expanded perspective

Suicide is Universal

Suicide is universal. Most everyone has considered suicide—even in an abstract way—at one time or another. Almost every intelligent and sensitive client in my practice has held the thought, if only for a minute, in his/her mind. Think of those moments when you are heartbroken, feel unlovable and worthless, and see no reason to go forward; or those times when you are in such dire straits, stripped and broken, and nothing seems possible; or when you are facing a terrible illness, you might think, "What would it matter?"

As we have discussed in the preceding pages, there are countless reasons and circumstances that can bring a person to that place where suicidal thoughts walk across their screen. Suicide is a fact of life and a means to death.

In this chapter, we are going in search of an expanded perspective regarding death and, more specifically, suicide. We are going to explore the big picture and look at the role of the soul and how these considerations can widen our view about the finality of death and the permanence of suicide.

Exploring New Territories

We once thought the world was flat and the earth was the center of the universe. As we experience and learn more, we discover new territories of thought and consideration. We expand our consciousness and, as a result, see our lives in a new light. Our world is forever changing and, as a result, our perceptions also change.

In this chapter, we are exploring new territories. We will look at the eternal nature of the soul, wonder if death is the final frontier, and consider messages from the Other Side. We look at suicide from a multi-dimensional perspective.

These concepts have given me a deeper and more expansive understanding of life and death. I have found solace, peace, and healing with these perspectives. And because of this, I have included these thoughts for your consideration. There are many points of view on these topics. These thoughts are what resonate with my heart.

The Many Faces of Suicide

Suicide is many things.

Suicide is not a sin, from my point of view. Some religions espouse hellfire and damnation; others ponder the intention of the suicidal individual. Since I see all of us on a path to open our hearts, expand our consciousness, and operate from our Best or Higher Selves, I do not believe that the Divine—in any form or moniker—is looking to punish us for being human. The Divine is all about love—unconditional love—and helping each of us find the pathway to that conclusion. Individuals who take their life by suicide are not punished. (Quite frankly, haven't they lived through enough hell?) That is old school thinking to me. If you believe in heaven, they are in heaven. If you believe in past lives, their souls are being readied for their next assignment. Where we all can agree is that the soul has moved out of the constraints and limitations of the 3D world and moved to another non-physical dimension.

Suicide is not a crime. (For the record, suicide is no longer illegal in the Western world, where suicide has been decriminalized. There are, however, legal ramifications to assisted suicide and the like).[1]

---

[1] http://en.wikipedia.org/wiki/Assisted_suicide/.

Some say the weak choose suicide. I disagree. "Weak" is not the operative word here.

Suicide can be a tipping point of pain or shame, a plea for help, a response to mental illness and haywire neurochemistry, as well as the last gasp of despair and resignation. Suicide can also be an impulsive mistake, a planned ending of life, a shredded soul, the death of the ego, or the ultimate act of rage and fury. (That rage and fury is often our much wounded child-self battling mightily for control or screaming in enormous pain.)

Suicide can be a choice that we may or may not understand on the 3D level, such as a teaching tool for our loved ones or choosing to do profound work from the Other Side.

Suicide can be a part of our destiny, our soul path toward healing.

Suicide can be the result of soul loss.

Suicide can be a game-changer. After the loss of a loved one to suicide, your view on life changes. Life becomes more fragile, more precious, and more cherished. This holds true for those who have attempted suicide as well. For them, the attempt may lead to a spurt of fresh energy and a re-engagement with life.

And suicide is definitely a societal, and, therefore, a political and moral issue. We human beings—and our organizations, corporations, or governments—can be terribly self-serving, ruthless, abusive, and tyrannical toward others. Acts of violence, war, and exploitation damage and destroy the very souls of our being. We lose ourselves and the meaning of our lives. Suicidal thoughts and actions are a part of the collateral damage of these polarizations.

Further, suicide can be a powerful teacher. It teaches us the great lesson of compassion. It opens us in ways we never thought possible. Suicide asks us to accept a loved one's choice and circumstance. Suicide asks us to forgive ourselves for our perceived wrongdoings, including our inability to prevent our loved one from harm. Suicide requires us to face our guilt, anger, and shame. Suicide asks us to accept the unacceptable, the inconceivable, the horrific, and make peace with it. Suicide asks us to live with an open heart. This means no judgment, no castigation, and no punishment. We see one another through a lens of acceptance. We allow each other to be who we are—in all of our shortcomings and crazy-making ways as well as all of our idiosyncratic wonderfulness.

A Word about Death

Death makes most of us uncomfortable. It is unfamiliar and frequently shoved out of sight and buried in our consciousness. It is the monster under the bed—always lurking and ready to grab us unexpectedly at a moment's notice. Death is scary and we generally avoid it at all costs.

The very *idea* of dying can make us feel uneasy. Will dying be painful, terrifying, or peaceful? Will I have lost my faculties, my loved ones, or my dignity? Will I be alone, in a hospital, or on the street? Sanitized thoughts of death—and life, too—are the preferred *modus operandi* for most of us. It's a protective mechanism.

Yet, counter to all of our strong-willed desires to live and seemingly antithetical to the very drive of human spirit, suicide is chosen. It is a self-inflicted death. Death is embraced and it arrives front and center in an unexpected and, often, very messy way. Suicide is seen, at that particular moment in time, to be the best option and the only response for the suicidal individual. The very human fear of dying is outweighed by the release from death and the end of pain.

When we think of death, we generally think *The End*, fade to black. There is nothing more. We have walked through the final exit door and had our last spin on the merry-go-round of life.

But what if there is more? What if death is not the end? What if death is a doorway to another experience in being?

Is Death the Final Frontier?

Steve Jobs called death "life's change agent." I agree. The death or end of any experience leads us to a new way of being, doing, or thinking. Death changes us. I often refer to death as a "fine-tune focuser of life" because death makes us see with new eyes. We don't take for granted what we once did. Our lives become less robotic and automatic. Our loved ones become even more precious. We move out of our heads and into our hearts.

Jobs saw death as a clearing agent "to make way for the new." I suspect he meant new people and new ideas. I totally concur that death is, indeed, a precursor to the new—and, in this case, a stepping-stone to the next level of soul development. Death is like a commencement ceremony; it takes us to a new platform of being.

Elisabeth Kübler-Ross felt similarly: "I've told my children that when I die, to release balloons in the sky to celebrate that I graduated. For me, death is a graduation."

If we move away from the black-and-white concept of either/or—that is, either life or death—let's consider what I call the spectrum of life and death. Your birth, coming into life, is one part of the spectrum. Your death, exiting life, is another part of the spectrum. And dotted along this spectrum, like so many sparkling lights, are the many births and deaths, entrances and exits, of your soul life. From this perspective, there is no finality in death. It is one of many exits leading to a new entrance.

Death makes way for a new beginning. To borrow a word from the shamanic tradition, death is simply another "shape shift" for our soul, from one kind of being to another. In other words, when we die, we drop the robe of our physical self and our soul moves forward for more experiences of service or those that lead to more soul growth.

The Soul is Eternal

The soul is our unique spark, our animating life force that we carry within our physical beings. Our bodies are temporal—in other words, time-limited—and when we die, our body no longer functions; whereas, our souls are eternal; they last forever. I refer to the soul as the "God Spark." It is the catalyst to life, creativity, and inspiration.

Our souls give us life. Loved ones and hospice nurses who have been at the bedside of a dying person will tell you that they have experienced moments of awareness when there is a discernible shift of energy, color, or light when the soul leaves the body at death.

We can define our souls as our particular incandescence. Like the filament in a light bulb, our soul is how we shine our version of light in the world.

And what does light look like? It looks like kindness, compassion, creativity, joy, goodness, gratitude, generosity, freedom, fighting for the underdog, standing up for the victimized, teaching, tending, lending a helping hand, sharing, awe, wonder, love, acceptance, and all of those feelings that uplift us, open our hearts, and connect us. When we operate from our sparkle, we feel whole and, sometimes, even larger than life.

Pierre Teilhard de Chardin was a French philosopher, paleontologist, and a Jesuit priest who said, "We are not human beings having a spiritual experience. We are spiritual beings having a human experience." And this statement is the crux of everything. In our humanness, we think we are merely human—limited, flawed, imperfect, and mortal. We do not recognize, much less factor in, that we are a lot like Clark Kent in that there is a magnificent, eternal soul beneath our everyday exterior.

The Afterlife

Do you remember the Frank Capra movie, *It's a Wonderful Life*? James Stewart plays the lead character, George Bailey, who reluctantly stays in his hometown to run the family business. Due to some family mishaps, George becomes despondent, drunk, and wishes he had never been born. George throws himself off a bridge and is rescued by Clarence the angel, who shows George what life would have been like for his family and friends if George had not been born. Upon reviewing his "unborn" life, George understands the difference he has made in the lives of his loved ones. Despite impending disaster and failure, George runs home, giddy with love for everyone and everything in his hometown.

I think the afterlife is a bit like that.

The way I understand it is this: When we die, we have a life review. We look at the life we have lived from the soul perspective. This is always unconditionally accepting and loving. Our version of Clarence the angel says something like, "Let's roll the video," and we experience, from a soul level, a review of our life. This is not a punitive measure to determine blame, nor to judge right or wrong, success or failure. This is a soul assessment of our life, seen with detachment and compassion. What were our choices? What kind of person have we been? Have we acted with kindness and generosity of spirit? Have we been able to forgive, apologize, or right a wrong? Did we share ourselves? In essence, have we acted with a good heart and grown closer to understanding that we are all connected, we are all one?

There is the story of the man who had a near-death experience (NDE) in which he traveled as far as his life review. He came back to life and his friend asked him what he had learned. He answered, "I should have been kinder."

This reminds me of ancient Egyptian mythology. Upon death, the heart, considered the home of the soul, was weighed against the lightness of the goddess Maat's feather. Her feather symbolized truth, justice, and balance. This was the measure of a life, a light or heavy heart, and this determined the outcome of the soul in the afterlife.

Reincarnation and Soul Contracts

Whether our souls are found heavy or light in this lifetime, they usually move along the wheel of life for another turn of experience.[2] This is called reincarnation.

Reincarnation is a subject of research, a topic of debate, an integral part of the Hindu and Buddhist traditions, and a personal memory for many individuals.

After the physical death, a soul experiences a new way of being and is reborn— that is, reincarnates—into a new life. The soul may incarnate in many possible configurations as it recycles through various lifetimes for the purpose of soul growth and service, which happens through the various relationships, interests, work experiences, studies, passions, and acts of service in the reincarnated soul's life.

In one lifetime, perhaps, you are Persian, in another, maybe, you are Roman. You have been male and female. You have died young; you have lived a long life. You have experienced different cultures, genders, body types, predilections, religions, races, politics, ideologies, states of health, degrees of beauty, and levels of social strata. You could have had or lost status, wealth, and power. You could have known great happiness, abject poverty, war, prison, travel, court life, or slavery. You could have been a thief, a murderer, or a rapist. You could have saved a child, ministered to the sick, or invented something revolutionary. In each lifetime, you have died in a different way—old age, illness, suicide, murder, war, betrayal, plague, and the like. Throughout these reincarnations, you have experienced life in a multitude of ways. And "different" is the operative word, because it is through these diverse and dissimilar lifetimes, your soul has evolved and expanded in consciousness.

The soul reincarnates to expand consciousness, experience different aspects of being, be of service, and to fulfill soul contracts.

To me, the concept of soul contracts is akin to the idea of destiny. They are like neighboring shades on the color palette. Destiny or fate is a predetermined course of events, whereas, soul contracts are predetermined energies that we, as a soul, agree to experience in a specific lifetime.

---

[2] Souls may choose to do their work in other dimensions.

Soul contracts are agreements made pre-incarnation. Our soul says, "Yes, please, I want to come in as the person who experiences . . ."—and you can fill in the blank as to what the lessons might be. Perhaps, it might be to learn from betrayal, overcome victimhood, understand self-worth, learn compassion, or know war. And all the parties involved in the "lesson" metaphorically raise their hands and say yes to their part of the soul growth experience. And when we incarnate, we immediately forget these soul contracts. We jump into human form and meet up with family and friends who can punch our buttons, stretch our hearts, or immediately feel like our long-lost twin. As one client kiddingly said to me, "Next time, I want to read the fine print in my contract before I sign on the bottom line."

Soul contracts imply that every meaningful relationship, whether good or not-so-good, is an important part of our soul path. Relationships are, in fact, our greatest spiritual teachers because through our interactions with one another, we learn about ourselves, inside and out. We learn how to stand up for ourselves, speak our truth, give freely, feel deeply, connect fully, grieve mightily, react crazily, become jealous or generous, jaded or possessive. We learn about betrayal, the power of example, abandonment, honor, dishonor, forgiveness, and acceptance. We learn how to enable, compromise, smother, abuse, manipulate, rage, create, inspire, and, of course, love.

Relationships, in a word, are key to learning about ourselves and choosing how we want to be in the world. And within the context of past lives, just think of the enormous number of relationships we have experienced in order to learn all the dimensions of the human heart and eternal soul.

Suicide, the Soul, and Reincarnation

From a soul perspective, suicide is simply a choice—not good, not bad, not right, not wrong. It is simply a choice. Contrary to many metaphysical teachings, there is no additional weight or baggage attached to the suicided soul.

Suicide is frequently the result of a lost or broken soul, a soul that has been pounded by crushing, often unimaginable, life experiences. Think of the soldiers and veterans who return from war; they are carrying the atrocities they endured, acted upon, and witnessed within their very beings. It can be more than one can bear.

An Irish therapist told me the story of an IRA terrorist who killed his co-worker. In an interview, the man said he physically felt his soul leave his body shortly after committing the murder. He admitted that he never felt whole again and later, as a result, he took his own life. Being soul-less is a shadow kind of existence. It's as if the light has been turned off and you feel hollow, lost, adrift, and dead inside.

We know that in ancient Rome and Japan, soldiers who lost in battle took their lives as a point of honor as well as to avoid potential torture by the enemy. From a reincarnation perspective, any one of us could have been one of those soldiers who chose suicide. Therefore, is it unreasonable to suggest that many of us have experienced a death by suicide in a past life? It's an interesting thought, isn't it?

If you are open to the idea of reincarnation, welcome to the concept of karma. The theory is that everything we do, including suicide, has karmic consequences. You know the expression, "What goes around, comes around." In other words, on a soul level, our every action will eventually balance out through various reincarnations. That is the Law of Karma:

"Every action generates a force of energy that returns to us in like kind. . . . What we sow is what we reap."[3]

I believe that on a soul level, our choices and actions are not good or bad, but simply paths of experience and wisdom. Some paths—and they are all soul-chosen—are certainly harder than others.

Some traditions believe that a suicide truncates soul growth, and so the karmic consequence will be that more "school-of-life lessons" are required of the soul. This makes no sense to me. Isn't the point of every soul to have life lessons?

I am all for reincarnation, but I find the karma concept to be a little heavy-handed with foreboding overtones.[4] There is a bit of a punitive implication, as if you will forever be doing *samsara* (the ongoing cycle of birth, death, and rebirth) on the wheel of karma because of your humanness. I can almost hear the Karmic Wheel Master say to me, *"You, back to cleaning the dungeon."*[5] This idea makes me laugh because I perceive the soul life to be so much more expansive and of a high-vibratory nature. However, if the gods want to send me back as the dog in my sister's household, sign me up.

---

3 http://www.chopra.com/community/online-library/the-seven-spiritual-laws-of-success/the-law-of-karma-or-cause-and-effect/.

4 I have heard spiritual teachers say that if you want to get off the wheel of karma and find enlightenment, you must have a guru. This concept is not for me.

5 Yes, I am being playful here, and I made up the Karmic Wheel Master.

Seriously, the punitive punch of any spiritual or religious teaching seems contrary to the whole purpose of soul evolution.

We know from child-rearing studies that punishment provokes fear, models aggression, impedes social development, impacts cognitive function, and can emotionally stunt a child. Punishment—by anyone or anything—sounds like a very effective distancing technique.

Years ago, there was an experiment done by energy workers on simple house plants. If you were in Group A, you yelled and cursed at the plants, and subsequently the plants withered and died. If you were in Group B, you spoke lovingly to the plants and they blossomed and grew. I suspect that a loving Divine Intelligence would be in Group B. Pounding on a human soul doesn't seem to be the fastest way to soul growth.

I believe that upon death, the ego is shed along with our robe of skin, and the soul is cleared and healed and prepped for the next assignment. There is no finger-wagging or foot-stomping or sharpening the guillotine for the soul. No matter how wonderful or atrocious a person was in his or her lifetime, the soul had raised its hand for the incarnation and the inherent experiences. The soul was simply doing its preordained job. (And yes, we have free will and we get to choose how we will respond to what is before us.)

Remember, suicide is not a "bad" soul choice; it is simply a choice, founded on many contributing factors.

One point to consider is intentionality. What was the intention in taking one's life? Was it to harm another? Usually not; more commonly, the intention is to get out of pain, stop the screaming inner voices, and end the misery. To me, we are talking about a population of seemingly broken souls—broken by genetics, biological vulnerabilities, and circumstances.

But what is the intention of the soul? You know the body may be fragile and the soul can be very strong.

These souls may very well have raised their soul "hands" to be enormous teachers to all of us supposedly "normal" ones. Perhaps, as unbelievable as it may sound, our loved one chose suicide for a higher purpose for us. Has our loved one's suicidal death stretched us wide open with compassion? Has it moved us to a new way of being? Has it helped us become less judgmental? It is something to ponder.

Another possibility is that the individual knew they were complete with their 3D life. This is usually the case with a mature soul.

There is the story of a Catholic priest from a number of years ago. He was considered a mystic by his fellow priests and colleagues. He had reached the point in life when he felt complete and certain that he had done all that he could do on the earth plane. He told his superiors he was going to consciously end his life because he had more work to do on the Other Side. They honored his actions and allowed him to be buried in sacred ground—an unheard of action at that point in time in the twentieth century.

Remember the story of my friend and colleague, Susan? Susan had cleared the decks, so to speak, in her life. She, too, was ready to do her work from the Other Side.

From a soul perspective, everything is not as it may seem on the human level.

A Mother's Belief: Saving Grace, by Grace Benz

I believe having a spiritual foundation and belief in a return to our heavenly home where peace can be found is a saving grace and brings comfort to our grief. That is definite!

I believe we must go through all our feelings, both "good" and "negative," to heal and clear and work through until we find resolve. . . . None can be avoided in order to find peace and balance.

Forgiveness of self and others is paramount in the healing process. I found that writing out a statement of forgiveness for myself and writing it 70 times for 7 days was extremely beneficial for me. My personal statement was, "I forgive myself for not being able to help my son, Chris." It may even need to be repeated again later on as part of the release process. I know, for me, as I cried and I wrote, I began to experience a weight being lifted from me that made a huge impact.

I also believe that if I can't get over the grief and pain and lift it up to a place that brings me peace and appreciation, then my loved one is held back at an emotional level that must be completed and therefore is unable to go on to fulfill the next stage of his journey into the higher dimensions.

I believe we must see death as another side of life and trust in the divine plan of All Creation. Love is the only thing that matters in the end, and often that is most starkly experienced when someone we LOVE so much passes away. Although our time is over, with LOVE there are no regrets, only gratitude, because LOVE is never lost, love never dies.

Death makes it real clear to those who remain with pain in their hearts, longing for the one who has passed away.

A part of me died when I lost my son, Chris (as he is truly a part of me and I him) and, yet, another part of me also ascended. In a way he took the fall for all of us to wake up and pay more attention to our relationships with each other. I can see it as a tragedy in 3D reality as well as a gift on a spiritual or in the greater reality. I believe that every challenge brings opportunity to grow, to transform to something better, to heal, to understand and to expand our spiritual growth. That was made very clear to me through the dream state which also gave me much healing and comfort. For the first three years, I dreamed of Chris every night. We talked, we hugged, and we interacted at every age level, like we were able to experience life once again in dreamtime.

I personally feel that death is always by choice. Whether you die in an "accident," from an illness, combat, murder, suicide, or whatever circumstance it may be, you have made that choice on a spiritual level. There have been many cases where people who have had near-death experiences have said they were told to go back because it wasn't their time yet or were given the option to choose. I believe we make soul contracts in order to help each other grow, expand, and learn the life lessons that we choose to accomplish while incarnate.

Anything that is not love becomes a burden to carry.

Does the Soul Remember?

There is much research being done around past-life memories and experiences. People undergo past life regressions with trained regression therapists or they have spontaneous memories. Perhaps, they have knowledge or a skill set for which they were not trained or a huge fear without any rational basis. Or they meet someone with whom they have a meaningful connection that feels timeless and familiar. There are those moments of *déjà vu* when you are certain you have previously experienced what is seemingly new to you now. It can be disconcerting because it is all too familiar. You have never done this; you have never been here; and you have never seen this before. How did you know that the bakery in Prague was on that little street? How did you know how to repair an antique lock?

In my own life, I remember as a girl of about 11 years of age traveling with my grandmother, mother, sister, and aunt. We were having lunch at a restaurant that was outside, on a tiled patio, atop a mountain. I was quietly freaking out, as I had a distinct memory of being there before. My sister, then a brother, had fallen off the mountain and I, also a male, was desperately trying to hold onto his hand and pull him up to safety. I vividly remembered how he had slipped out of my hand and fell, presumably to his death. I had never been to this part of the world before, and what I felt was exceedingly real and visceral.

I have a godchild who has never lived near the ocean in her life. However, since she was quite small—and up to the present day—she has had a huge terror of being eaten by a shark.

Where do these feelings come from? I think the soul remembers.

Messages from the Other Side[6]

Throughout time and across the vast cultural spectrum, people have acknowledged, felt, or heard the whisper of their deceased loved ones and ancestors. For many, it is not considered an unusual phenomenon, but rather a normal and regular part of daily life. It is accepted and welcomed. For others, this idea of communication with the dead seems preposterous. And that was the way I was raised: no one talked to the dead, unless you counted praying to the saints or your guardian angel.

However, over the years, all of this has changed for me. It happened in small increments. There would be the sense of someone with me—riding in the passenger seat of the car, trailing me up a flight of stairs, or walking next to me. There could be pervasive lingering scents associated with someone who had passed. There was a period of time when I had frequent night visitations. This included two young men who had been killed in a car accident sitting in my rocking chair. In conversations with others about their grief, images of their deceased loved one might appear on my inner screen and occasionally would be accompanied by a sense of words to communicate. And, in 2005, while in Gulfport, Mississippi, as a Red Cross volunteer following Hurricane Katrina, I had multiple experiences of connecting with the Other Side, experiences that totally erased any lingering doubts and confirmed for me that communication with the Other Side is real.

---

[6] More examples are given in a 2007 piece, Messages from the Other Side www.religionand-spirituality.com/view/post/11798948370900/.

Generally, I have found that those who have communicated from the Other Side are filled with affection and care. They want to help us, remind us, and even protect us. They may want to apologize, ask for forgiveness, and seek a peaceful resolution. Most often, they connect with us from a place of expanded soulfulness and unconditional love.

Those of us who grieve hold our deceased loved ones closely in our hearts. They live there forever. They are always real in that sense. I proffer the possibility that there is more to consider—there is a spirit realm teeming with activity and a willingness to connect and communicate.

The Messages Continue

While writing this book, an intuitive colleague, who is also a physician, told me that I was surrounded by a number of spirits. All of my conversations around suicide had roused the dead, so to speak, and a number of these deceased (by suicide) loved ones were vying for my attention. They had things to say. My colleague likened my energy to that of Whoopi Goldberg's character, Oda Mae Brown, in the 1990 movie, *Ghost*.

Visitors from the other realms are not new to me, but I was so busy dealing with the 3D world of the book, I was not paying close attention to what I had been experiencing.

In hindsight, I realized I would find myself staring—with greater and greater frequency—at the carpet on the floor, the tiles on the shower wall, and the greenery outside my windows. And, while staring, everything morphed into a face, and sometimes many faces all lined up as if in a composite picture frame. I knew from previous experiences that I was moving into spontaneous trance states. Further, I had been experiencing a number of headaches and on/off feelings of vertigo. I was feeling off-balance, literally and metaphorically.

Once the dots were connected for me, I opened the curtain for their communication, and this is what I have heard:

~   I love you, darling.

~   There is a time and place for everything. This was my time. I'm fine. Truly. Fine.

~   Don't waste your life crying over me, it's spilt milk.

~   I feel your love. Thank you.

~ Don't hate me. I did the best I could.

~ You're doing such good work. I'm so proud of you.

~ Get on with your life, don't stew in the past.

~ It really is me in your dreams.

~ I didn't want to hurt you, but I had to leave. I couldn't live with myself anymore.

~ Go and live life. It's your turn now.

~ It was over, so over.

~ I was too sad.

~ Can you ever forgive me?

~ It was too hard.

~ I got carried away, I didn't mean for it to happen.

~ I'm working hard [from the Other Side].

~ Don't be mad at me. I wasn't as strong as you thought.

~ I couldn't do it anymore.

~ I wasn't going to take anybody out with a car accident and there was no illness for me to claim; suicide was the easiest way for me to be free.

~ Please forgive me and go be happy.

~ It's so much better now. It's easier when you are out of the body. It was my time to go.

~ Remember me with kindness.

~ Think of me with love.

~ Remember the days we had fun. Remember how we laughed.

~ I love you always.

~ It's over now; get on with living your life. Have fun with the kids. Get married again. I want you to be happy. You did nothing wrong.

The veil between the worlds is thinner and more porous than we might imagine. I believe that we have loved ones who have passed over, and they are cheering for us and wanting us to have the best possible life experiences, especially after the pain of their passing.

A Message for You, from Gary

I had sensed there was more to be revealed. I received this message[7] from a young man who lost his life through suicide. This is a message for those who wonder why they should stay on the planet when everything is so hard and difficult.

A Message from Gary

Yea, my name is Gary. No need to doubt it. Let's get on with what I have to say.

I killed myself. Life was too hard. Who cared about me? Nobody loved me. Nobody understood me. I had no real girl to call my own. My family was a mess. I was locked in my own bubblehead, feelin' all pitiful and sorry about me.

I hated myself. And I hated everything around me. I didn't trust anyone. I didn't believe anyone. I didn't even trust myself. Everything was just more crap. What was there to hope for? As if I could ever make the kind of money it takes to live a big life. I was doomed from the get-go.

I was a regular guy from a regular neighborhood. I would walk in the alley behind the houses. I'd meet my friends there and then we'd go hang out. Our lives were nothing. We'd do stupid and dumb jackass stuff. There was a mangy dog who hung out by the garbage cans in the alley, I liked him. He always was scrounging for some food and somebody to horse around with. We were both kind of desperate. I wanted to feel important. Be a big man and show everybody that I had the goods. I thought that was the answer.

I stole a little. I drank some. I smoked and tried anything I was given. I wanted out of myself. I didn't want my f'ing existence. I wanted to be the cool king of the neighborhood with a fistful of cash, girls dripping off me, and every-body wanting to be me.

Home was a nightmare. My mother was a part-time lush; my father even worse. He was angry all the time. Yelling, screaming, hitting, it didn't matter what, he just start whaling on me or my brother. Worse than the beatings were

---

[7] This message came in several installments and has been edited for clarity and continuity.

the things he used to call me. I was just shit on his shoes. It was different when I was a little kid. Then, my mom was sweet and my dad wasn't so mean.

I got into gambling. It was a rush to make fast money, but I started losing big, and the guys beat me up worse than my father ever did. I stopped. Then, my mom got real sick.

I took my life by gunshot wound. It seemed the best way to do it. Best. No pain. Reliable as long as I kept my hand steady, and I did.

Why did I do this?

I saw no reason to live. What was the point? My life didn't seem to matter to anyone. My life was shit. My friends turned on me. They didn't like me anymore. My girlfriend turned on me. Everybody thought I was the bad guy. I was f'd up. My parents didn't see it. They were busy with their own lives. My sister was young and my brother was away from home. I acted like everything was normal, but on the inside I was a rolling mess. Felt kinda bad, but it [suicide] seemed like my only answer. There was no reason to keep living.

After I died, they were all real sad.

After I died I went to another kind of place. It was peaceful. I didn't feel bad about anything. Something happened. I'm different now. I got clear after I died. I am not miserable anymore. You want to kill yourself, go ahead. But if you ask me why you should stay alive, here's what I've got to say:

You think you're going to solve your problems, but you won't really if you killed yourself for the reasons I did. I shot myself because I thought I was no good. I was a piece of shit. No reason to live. Who would care? I certainly didn't.

I see things differently now. I didn't really understand this soul stuff. I have the soul and it's a pretty good part of me. It's bigger than feeling shitty. If I stayed on the planet now, I could help. I could make a difference. I was good at drawing and how to figure out things to build. I missed my chance to be a warrior. I could've fought for some good stuff like ecology or building houses. My soul could have made a difference. I did not realize I carried that kinda potential.

I get it now, we're all connected. When I left, I left my family and friends and others I have not met yet. I left a hole. Through a bunch of lifetimes we have been together. We were all part of something bigger. How come nobody teaches this stuff?

I want to say to anybody listening, don't give up. You are worth something. You just don't know it yet. They beat you down pretty hard and it can be really bad, but there's so much more.

There's a fight going on between light and dark on earth. Don't let the dark, the Voldemorts,[8] *suck the life out of you. Hang in there. It can get better when you realize that you are more than your shitty life. It can come out when you do creative stuff. Create whatever you want. Everybody's got something. I don't necessarily mean painting and stuff. Find something you really like and go for it.*

People are too mean. Don't let them put you down.

I want you to stop and think about what you are planning. You may not believe it but there will be tears shed when you die. It's not random that you're here. You're here for a reason. It's what your soul decided to do. Your soul work is why you are here. Like I said, I could have been a warrior. Fight a good cause and taken all my anger and funneled it into something different. Think I probably would have felt better, too, if I just did something that felt like it mattered. So, you, do something different. Don't be stuck. Change it up.

Your life is important. You are a part of the plan. Your soul is your light and that's your contribution to the planet. Your light is necessary because there is a battle with the dark. Don't let the dark ones eat you alive. Don't do it. You be you. You be here. You do something, anything that makes you feel good to be alive, ok? You will actually feel better in the long run if you stay.

Thanks for listening.

---

[8] This is a reference to the fictional character Lord Voldemort, the leader of the Dark Ones in J. K. Rowling's *Harry Potter* series of books.

I'll try to be around and about. But if I'm not,
then you know that I'm behind your eyelids,
and I'll meet you there.

—Terence McKenna

Everybody dies. There's nothing you can do about it.
Whether or not you eat six almonds a day.
Whether or not you believe in God.
(Although there's no question a belief in God
would come in handy. It would be great to think there's a
plan, and that everything happens for
a reason. I don't happen to believe that. And every time
one of my friends says to me, 'Everything
happens for a reason,' I would like to smack her.)

—Nora Ephron, *I Remember Nothing: and Other Reflections*

Memories are of the ethereal,
and not the material world,
that is how I know I am forever.

—Michael Poeltl

Just as when we come into the world,
when we die we are afraid of the unknown.
But the fear is something from within us
that has nothing to do with reality.
Dying is like being born: just a change.

—Isabel Allende, *The House of the Spirits*

Chapter Eleven

The energy of suicide

Jumping Ship

W hy are so many people choosing to leave right now? The numbers of people across the globe who are jumping ship and leaving Planet Earth seem astonishing. The number of suicides speaks to a bigger picture.

The death of the ego, the epidemic of soul loss, robotic lives, and battling polarities are part of this overriding energy. Allow me to explain.

Understanding the Death of the Ego

Psychologically speaking, the death of the ego, as the name suggests, is the death of how we see, identify, and name ourselves. We let go of our old ways of being and become someone new. Sometimes, we change by choice; other times, our life experiences shape our perceptions of ourselves. With the death of our ego, our belief systems become irrevocably altered, and we see ourselves and our place in the world with new eyes.

We all experience deaths of the ego as we walk through life and have new roles and experiences. This is a natural outgrowth of our maturing and evolving selves. This happens to us when we experience significant life transitions and seminal events such as the change of status and responsibilities brought about by new parenthood, marriage, divorce, widowhood, illness, bankruptcy, huge financial windfall, a big promotion, military service, graduating college, significant grief and loss, unemployment, and the like. These experiences (coupled with new, enlarged, or decreased levels of responsibility) modify how we perceive ourselves and our place in the world. This death of the ego, predicated on life changes, is not uncommon. We let go of the old ways of thinking and doing—the ways that no longer serve us—and we morph into our new way of being.

However, if we are resistant and fearful of change, we may consciously or unconsciously choose to stay stuck in the past. Further, there are also occasions when our ego becomes stuck and rutted in a certain role or archetypal way of being that initially brought us pleasure and satisfaction. The role of caregiver is a prime example. When we reach the place where we feel imprisoned by the very lives we have chosen, we want to break out of our self-constructed prison and be free of our old ways. We no longer want to walk, talk, and be this way in the world. Hence, there is a death of the outdated ego as we change our relationship with ourselves and the world.

After suffering from bouts of depression and suicidal thoughts, author Eckhart Tolle says he totally changed his perception of himself in the world following an epiphany in which he perceived ego, thought, and consciousness in a new way.

The ego can also look like a wounded, unhealed child-self (in an adult body) who, for example, has temper tantrums, is totally egotistical, forever a victim, a bully, or one who constantly rages. If childhood wounds are healed, the person grows in consciousness and moves through a death of the old ego structure and onto another platform of being served by this new, healthier ego structure.

Years ago, I worked with a successful corporate attorney. He had been totally irresponsible throughout his adolescence and early college days. He assumed his intelligence would bring him success, even if he was an angry, defiant "screw-off" and flunking out of community college. He realized with a sudden slap of clarity that if he did not change his ways, his future options were limited. With this realization, he acted anew and achieved a 4.0 GPA, transferred to a bigger college, and the rest, as they say, is history. Through his strong will, this man consciously "killed" his old self and birthed his new self—another example of a death of the ego.

The death of the ego is an ongoing life occurrence. Significant life events change all of us on a regular and consistent basis, and, in turn, we reconfigure how we see ourselves and our place in the world. This is a psychological cycle of death and rebirth.

Suicide and the Death of the Ego

Suicide is the ultimate death of the ego. There are two possible interpretations of suicide from this perspective: psychological and spiritual.

The death of the ego from a psychological perspective suggests someone who cannot move beyond the wounded self. Their actions may be aggressive, hostile, abusive, and defiant. Their thinking may be truncated, circular, irrational, and argumentative. The combination of an unhealed wounded self plus triggering life experiences, some of which may include addiction and impulsivity, can result in suicidal thinking or actions. Think of the chronically angry person who is defiant, emotionally shut down, abuses substances, feels victimized by the world, and can be dangerously impulsive. When this person crosses a threshold of rage and pain, there can be a high probability of suicide. The same can happen with the heartbroken person who feels alone, unworthy, and drowning in a disconnected darkness. They are straitjacketed in their wounds and unable to feel or find hope or possibility.

The second type of a suicidal death of the ego relates to the soul. This suicide physically resembles other suicides, but the underlying *raison d'être* is about a soul choice. This death of the ego is completed by those who have readily and willing dropped their ego and chosen suicide for a higher good. They have raised their hands, so to speak, to do work from the Other Side in service for humanity. Their suicide is the result of soul evolution. The death of their ego is also the death of their body. It is a release from the physical dimensions, and their soul is now free to work from the vastness of being. My friend Susan, the psychologist, is a good example of a suicidal death of the ego. Her soul has gone on to do good work from the nonphysical plane (as told to me in messages from the Other Side).

There has been an increase of the "raised-hands" suicides during recent years because many souls have volunteered to work on behalf of humankind in this way. Their work is aiding and abetting the shift in consciousness, as we move toward a more unified, heartfelt, and connected way of being.

Suicide is an Epidemic

Suicide is more than mental health and addiction; it is a global epidemic.

An epidemic is defined as a widespread occurrence of an infectious disease. It becomes an epidemic when the outbreaks or numbers exceed the expectations based on recent experiences.[1] The current suicide statistics are alarming. I think we would all agree that these numbers have exceeded our expectations.

Suicide is certainly infectious in its reach. The taboo has been broken. Suicide has become more commonplace. The idea has spread and seeds itself in our most vulnerable and wounded as a viable option to end their pain and disconnection.

One Southern California sheriff told a surviving loved one that he has attended more suicide calls than ever before. He has almost become numb to it, as the tragedies are so overwhelming. Suicide is everywhere—from boardroom to classroom, from war-weary soldiers to bankrupt farmers, from the homeless to the brain injured, from the disadvantaged to the disenfranchised. There is rarely a corner of life that is not touched by suicide. Even child prodigies deal with thoughts of suicide.[2]

Suicide speaks to an overall societal gestalt. And I think we could safely call this overriding pattern of functioning a "dis-ease," and the primary etiology is soul loss.

Suicide and Soul Loss

Our society is ill. We just need to look at our world. Where do we place our values and our priorities? "Should children have plastic surgery?" was a question on a morning show. We are out of balance and off-kilter. Our priorities are upside down. Our idolization of money, power, fame, and physical perfection are our tin gods. We compare ourselves and always come up short.

We are disconnected from ourselves, and this means we are disconnected from our souls. We are over-caffeinated, sleep-deprived, and grow dependent on alcohol,

---

[1] http://en.wikipedia.org/wiki/Epidemics; *Principles of Epidemiology*, 2nd edition (Atlanta: Centers for Disease Control and Prevention).

[2] Andrea Sachs, The Downside of Being a Child Prodigy, *TIME* magazine, September 6, 2006, content.time.com/time/arts/article/0,8599,1532087,00.html/.

recreational drugs, and/or pharmaceuticals. We are tethered to our electronic devices 24/7.

Time is the anathema. There is no time to be. We run pell-mell through our days, through our lives, trying to keep everyone happy and food on the table and making sure homework is done. Doing is the overarching call of the day. And society, as a whole, marches in lockstep toward yet another deadline, goalpost, project, chore, or activity to complete.

There is precious little time to cultivate a soul life where we might feed ourselves regular doses of beauty, nature, and quietude. Reflection, being in the moment, savoring the experience, and having a heartfelt conversation with our dear ones remain on our "to-do" lists.

The young suicides, in particular, speak to a tear in the fabric of society. What behavior are we modeling for them? Is life merely a race of accomplishment? Where are meaning, substance, and initiation into adulthood? They are so vulnerable to outside influences and have not been trained in developing an awareness of their soul, much less their energy body. Our young people have no understanding of their fullness.

And time stands still with trauma, which is, unfortunately, all too pervasive and leads to soul loss. Think of the military, weary after multiple deployments, with possible brain injuries, physical handicaps, and most likely PTSD. Many of their souls have been left wandering on the battlefield; they return home hollowed out from the horrific.

And there are the children. The studies indicate 1 in 5 girls and 1 in 20 boys are victims of childhood sexual abuse.[3] This leads to more unspeakable trauma and soul loss that can carry forward for generations if left untreated.

Perspectives shift in Indigenous tribes, where the shamans view Western diagnoses of mental illness as soul loss, spirit invasion, or some other event on the spiritual dimension.

Soul loss is everywhere. It is a product of our fast-paced, industrialized progress that runs as fast as it can. However, the running moves us away from our connections with ourselves and others. Life becomes too fast and frenetic, and we lose ourselves, displace our energies, and disconnect from our souls.

---

3 Studies by David Finkelhor, Director of the Crimes Against Children Research Center, as cited on http://www.victimsofcrime.org/library/crime-information-and-statistics/.

We have created a world that grows tighter and tighter and more and more constricted with supposed progress, all at the cost of humanity. And rampant suicide is a certainly a very large price to pay. The epidemic of suicide also speaks to the soul loss of our world at large.

Living Lives of the Living Dead

The Ancients would tell us, "As above, so below." In other words, the macrocosm reflects the microcosm, and vice versa, the microcosm reflects the macrocosm.

The soul loss that is evidenced in first-world nations and well-developed, industrialized countries reflects the soul loss of many an individual who is living a life of the living dead—or one could even say partial suicide. These are lives that are empty, rote, and without meaning.

Stress disorders, insomnia, workaholism, alcoholism, and any other "ism" we want add to the mix, reflect a soul-less life. Life is constantly on the run. Individuals feel powerless as they drive themselves harder and harder, faster and faster. Their pressure-cooker lives keep ratcheting up with more and more demands of time and energy, while the potential for explosion and disintegration hisses in the background.

Lives are fast, furious, and shockingly empty and robotic. We have forgotten how to stop and smell the roses. We are hunkered down in the trenches doing our thing, trying to survive, and taking care of what needs to be done. We have forgotten the play of sunlight on trees or moonlight on water. We have forgotten how to be happy, satisfied, and content. We often forget to be grateful. We are just so tired, so very, very tired from all that doing.

Our souls are depleted and frequently forgotten in the rush for survival. We yearn for time and space to simply be, to take in the healing balm of beauty and nature, and the good medicine of heart connections, laughter, and creativity. Our souls invite us to a life with meaning and substance and for moments of awe, reverence, and gratitude. We want to feel the connection with flowers, stars, and dolphins.

When we are fully plugged in and connected to our soul, we feel most alive, full, and appreciative. And the animated soul-life is the opposite of a numb, exhausted, half-lived, half-dead, airless life.

Dueling Polarities

Mother Earth is home of the universal push/pull of life and death, creation and destruction. We see these polarities reflected in abundance vs. poverty, greed vs. hunger, abuse vs. respect, birth vs. death, sacred vs. profane, soulful vs. soul loss, and in all conflicts, fights, and struggles. All of these tugs-of-war are representative of the larger whole. Every day we are seeing the battle of life and death or, more energetically described, the battle of light and dark being played out before us.

Polarities force a choice. You are right or wrong, good or bad, north or south, this or that, old or new. On the positive side, polarities can feed creativity, catalyze action, change world-views, form leaders, and create heroes. There is energy in choosing a side and taking a stand. You have used your heart, mind, and gut to form your decision. You rally to fight your cause, defend the underdog, and make your position known. It can feel righteous and honorable.

In light of history, we could easily argue that if we did not "fight the good fight,"[4] the world would be in a more terrible place and, possibly, even, non-existent. That may well be so. However, today's world seems more fractious than ever and hell-bent on winning at all costs, regardless of the collateral damage.

This reminds me of the 1989 movie *The War of the Roses*, in which a divorcing couple cannot agree on the terms of their divorce settlement. As a result, they destroy the very home they had so lovingly created over the course of their marriage. The film was billed as a black comedy. To me, it was heartbreaking that individuals could go to such extremes. The result was utter destruction.

Extreme polarities create enemies, feed conflict, feast on opposition, and narrow thinking. Extreme polarities put compassion on the back burner. Extreme polarities do not like compromise, bridge building, or making peace. There is only one right answer and it is theirs. These polarities are all about winning—period.

From a big-picture perspective, polarities obfuscate the fact that everything exists on a continuum, where everything is connected and everything is related. That said, one might also argue that these dueling polarities are the very runway to an understanding of oneness and unity.

From my perspective, our present, ongoing battle of light vs. dark represents our labor pains as we prepare for a new birth of a global shift in consciousness and

---

4 Attributed to St. Paul the Apostle.

awareness. Like the caterpillar that has morphed into the nascent butterfly, we, too, are metaphorically beating our wings to free ourselves from the cocoon of constriction and darkness.

The Energy of Suicide

Quantum physics teaches us that everything is energy and everything is related. We are all connected energetically. What happens to one of us happens to all of us.

From my perspective, currently there is an energy of suicide circling our globe. This energy is about choosing to die for many possible reasons.

What feeds this energy of suicide?

We are more aware of suicide—both globally and individually via the six-degrees-of-separation concept—than ever before. The sheer volume of suicides has an impact on all of us. The numbers also influence others who might be considering the option. There is a collective weight—the density of heartbreak—we all carry. We are altered by the loss of so many who were suffering in pain and have chosen suicide. Energetically, we are all connected and suicide is part of our collective (un)consciousness and is also in our energy fields. These suicides are part of us.

We know that soul loss is a contributing factor to suicide, and the epidemic of soul loss increases the weight of darkness and disconnection around us. Half-lived, half-dead lives are soul-less. These lives do not feed the light, because their light, their soul, has been dimmed by circumstances or repeated trauma. Henry David Thoreau said it best: "Most men lead lives of quiet desperation and go to the grave with the song still in them." Alas, this is true. There are too many unsung songs, and this also has enormous impact on the suicidal energy of the planet.

One of the most virulent factors that feeds the energy of suicide is the extreme dueling polarities. These energies leave little room for others. These energies aim to take you captive with fear. They want to hold you hostage with terror. You can find yourself paralyzed and afraid to move. These energies feed on the dark; they are the life-blood of PTSD and other traumas. These energies are highly contagious. They require your vigilance and mindfulness to avoid capture.

The suicidal death of the ego by the spiritually advanced serves as a counterweight to the darkness around suicide. It reminds us that suicide is not the Final Act of the soul. It reminds us that there is more to life than our 3D selves. It teaches us that suicide can also be an act of service and a part of the light.

The current suicidal energy on the planet is a symbol of our times as our collective whole works toward higher consciousness and unity. We all raised our respective soul hands to be here now, at this moment in history and at this moment of planetary evolution. The energy of suicide is a clarion call for us to heal our souls, honor our light, and connect with others in order to increase the amplitude on the planet.

Let's Not Declare War on Suicide, Let's Make Peace

Suicide is a not a target, or an adversary. It is an individual response to a confluence of factors.

If we want to address suicide, then we must sink down into the essentials and deal with the factors that contribute to suicide. And those factors are how we treat one another and ourselves. It is that basic.

Why not embrace differences, understand commonality, and reinforce the idea of oneness? We are all connected. Let's go for bridge-building. Let's develop our C.Q., our cultural quotient, so that we understand one another better. Let's make room at the table for everyone. We can agree to disagree, and we can find the common thread in our shared human experience.

Why not expand our perspective and provide tools? Let's raise our E.Q., our emotional quotient, and gain mastery. Let's become fluent in emotional intelligence so that we can talk to one another, express our anger, and deal with conflict in an effective way. We can have healthier relationships. Let's teach energy techniques and self-healing modalities, like HeartMath®, Reiki, Therapeutic Touch, and shamanism, for self-empowerment, resilience building, and an increased understanding of the power of personal energies.

Why not change our focus? We can increase cognitive dissonance around bullying, unethical behavior, and violence. We can work toward eradicating the learned responses of shame and fear. We can promote cooperation vs. competition; and we can make life-work-balance a priority. These are possibilities and options to create a healthier and happier society.

Speaking of priorities, how we treat our children says volumes about our societies. Let's feed, house, clothe, and educate our children. Why are any children on this globe going to bed hungry? Let's address childhood sexual abuse, sex trafficking, and domestic violence. Children are in crisis—and they are our future.

Let's share our burdens by practicing empathy and cultivating compassion. We need to walk in one another's shoes. Let's give our wounded the help they need. Mental health services, VA services, and the like are in dire need of public support and funding. Substance abuse requires more long-term treatment strategies. Why is this problematic?

And if we are to address the pervasive soul loss, then we need to honor the soul. We can move toward that by rebalancing priorities, respecting Mother Nature, healing Mother Earth, celebrating the arts, course-correcting the pace, being open to creative expression, and developing more meaningful ways of connecting with one another.

And, lastly, we need to live peace, with ourselves and with others. If we cannot accept ourselves, if we feel we are forever unworthy, we will act in ways that can have enormous ripple effects. Peace is a five-letter word that offers relief and healing. And it starts with each of us.

Shall we make a new rule of life from tonight:
always try to be a little kinder than is necessary.

—Sir James M. Barrie

The effect of one good-hearted person
is incalculable.

—Oscar Arias Sanchez

When the story of these times gets written,
we want it to say that we did all we could,
and it was more than anyone could have imagined.

—Bono

Appendix

Durkheim's Types of Suicide

*É*MILE DURKHEIM (1858–1917) was a French sociologist, social psychologist, philosopher, and the author of *Le Suicide* (1897). According to Durkheim, it is not the psychological force that determines suicide, but rather the social force, the relationship between the individual and society—that is, a person's social groupings.

Durkheim's categories are thus focused only on the social realm, and they lack the important physical and psychological influences, but they are still worth consideration. How we fit into the world, where we see our place in the world, how we connect and relate to others, and how others connect to us, matter enormously. We are social beings, and feeling alone, disconnected, and not of importance to anyone is very painful and a critical factor in suicidality.

1. *Egoistic suicide* is when a person does not feel connected to society and feels that he or she has no place in the world. There is isolation from the social group. There is no tether or anchor. This type of suicide is often a last-ditch resort of depression and isolation, and is found with increased frequency among unmarried males, among those in the military, and among veterans who have not managed to reintegrate into society.

2. *Altruistic suicide* is the opposite of egoistic suicide. This person has a high level of integration with society. Think of the Hindu custom where the wife throws

herself on her husband's funeral pyre, the young person who identifies whole-heartedly with a song, or the soldier who acts for the common good.

3. *Anomic suicide* comes from a situation of chaos and confusion, especially from social and economic upheaval. It occurs when the rules on how to behave with one another are breaking down, and individuals do not know where they fit or how to behave. Social norms are lacking. This can happen with extreme changes in economics, such as economic ruin, and even with windfalls. Examples would be the farmers in India with failed crops, and the suicides due to economic crises in Italy, Greece, and Ireland.

4. *Fatalistic suicide* is the opposite of the anomic suicide. In this instance, there is no chaos and confusion, but excessive social restraint. Think of the person who takes his or her life en route to prison, suicide by cop, or suicide to avoid an arranged marriage

Influencing Risk Factors and Stressors

Suicide is far-reaching. It is pervasive. It is global. Many factors can influence thoughts of suicide. It is never simply one thing.

You could have a problem with pain meds or alcohol and lose your job and, eventually, your housing. You could suffer from chronic depression and feel bio-chemically pinned to the mat when you get a serious medical diagnosis and the treatment bankrupts you. You could return from war with insomnia, raging night-mares, and no place to call home. You could be heartbroken after a break-up and feel you will never experience love again. You can no longer feed, support, or house your family. You become desperate. There are so many possible scenarios.

Accumulated stressors can make even the strongest person feel disempow-ered, full of shame, and without options. And for those who are more fragile and vulnerable because of their circumstance and/or genetics, suicide can seem like a way out of the misery. Yes, suicide is counterintuitive to our survival instinct, and it also speaks to the sheer force and magnitude of the pain, disconnection, and hope-lessness a person may feel.

If we are to address suicide, then it behooves us to understand the risk factors and psychosocial stressors that can trigger suicidal feelings and potential suicidal action. As poet John Donne said, "No man is an island . . . every man is a piece of the continent, a part of the main." In other words, we are all connected and what we do affects others. As Émile Durkheim suggested over 100 years ago, society does have a role in suicide.

In the following, you will find an overview of the risk factors and stressors that can prompt a range of suicidal actions. For a sense of organization, I have made eight general categories with specific examples. This list is not exhaustive, nor is it black and white. It is meant as a starting point.

Clearly, not everyone who experiences the risk factors listed will become suicidal. That said, stressors—economic, emotional, medical, mental health, physical, social, soul, and traumatic experiences and wounds—coupled with family history, genetic predispositions, and biochemical imbalances, can influence an individual's decision to take suicidal action, whether attempted or realized.

The intention of this list is to underscore the widespread reach of suicidal factors and to offer some understanding of why suicide is a far-too-common reality in today's world.

Economic issues

◆ Bankruptcy

◆ Debt collection (unrelenting and threatening)

◆ Farm failures

◆ Foreclosures

◆ Homelessness

◆ Student loans

Family history

◆ Mental illness

◆ Substance abuse

◆ Suicide

◆ Violence

Mental health disorders

◆ Bipolar disorder

◆ Borderline disorder

◆ Major depressive disorder

◆ Post-traumatic stress disorder (PTSD)

◆ Psychotic Disorders

◆ Schizophrenia

Physical issues

◆ Addiction

◆ Anorexia nervosa

◆ Chronic pain

◆ Chronic traumatic encephalopathy (CTE)

◆ Cluster headaches

◆ Organic brain disease

◆ Side effects from medications

◆ Terminal illness

◆ Traumatic brain injury (TBI)

◆ Trigeminal neuralgia

Psychological pain (severe and debilitating)

◆ Abandonment

◆ Anger

◆ Anxiety

◆ Complicated grief

◆ Despair

◆ Emotional and mental abuse, i.e., bullying, subjugation, etc.

- Failure
- Guilt
- Hopelessness
- Impulsivity and aggression (in conjunction with other mental health issues)
- Inability to forgive
- Multiple losses/trauma
- Prior suicide attempt
- Relationship issues, i.e., break-ups, betrayal, etc.
- Risk taking and impulsive behavior
- Self-harm
- Separation and disconnection
- Shame
- Shattered self-worth and feelings of worthlessness
- Unabated fear and terror
- Unresolved regret

Social issues

- Alienation of Indigenous peoples
- Breaking from cultural tradition and rules, i.e., forced marriages
- Copycat suicides
- Cult behavior and mob mentality
- Drugs
- Gun control
- Incarceration
- Influence of the media
- Intolerance, i.e., sexual preference, race, nationality, religion, gender, etc.
- Ostracism

- Religious and political dictates
- Suicide as a weapon of war
- Suicide by cop
- Torture
- Underage drinking
- Veteran support

Soul issues

- Karmic ruts
- Soul contracts
- Soul loss
- Spiritual crises

Trauma

- Acculturation and immigration difficulties
- Acts of terrorism
- Bullying
- Catastrophic illness
- Financial disaster
- Major accidents, i.e., airplane crash
- Natural disasters
- Sexual abuse, most notably, childhood sexual abuse
- Suicide of others (witnessing of a suicide or the aftermath of a loved one's suicide)
- Violence
- War

Resources

When you are on a healing path, it is helpful to have some resources as a jumping-off point for your journey. The following is certainly not an exhaustive compilation. It is intended to provide you with a place to start in areas that may be of interest or assist in your healing process. There is no one way to grieve, as there is no one way to heal. There are many diverse roads and avenues to explore. Hopefully, you will find something or someone in these listings that resonate with you and can aid and abet your journey.

You will find what I call "bibliotherapy," some good books to meet you where you are as well as give you some additional insight and information. There are self-help books, inspirational books, memoirs, novels, books for children, and, even a book of poetry. There are also online resources, including national organizations that can provide you with excellent support and further well-researched resources.

Good luck on your healing journey.

Bullying

Julia Cook, *Bully B.E.A.N.S.* (kids' book) (National Center for Youth Issues, 2009)

Walter G. Meyer, *Rounding Third* (MaxM Ltd, 2009). This novel received widespread news coverage, as it deals with teens being bullied until one attempts suicide. Meyer is an anti-bullying champion. www.waltergmeyer.com.

Coping with a Loss by Suicide

American Association of Suicidology, www.suicidology.org

>   Suicide support centers across the US, resources for suicide loss survivors and support for suicide attempt survivors.

American Foundation for Suicide Prevention, www.afsb.org

>   Funds research, education, and treatment programs aimed at the prevention of suicide; raises funds for research and visibility about suicide through "Out of the Darkness" walks.

Iris Bolton, with Curtis Mitchell, *My Son . . . My Son . . . A Guide to Healing after Death, Loss or Suicide* (Bolton Press, rev. ed., 1983)

Michelle Linn-Gust, PhD, www.inspirebymichelle.com

>   *Do They Have Bad Days in Heaven? Surviving the Suicide Loss of a Sibling* (Chellehead Works, 2001)

>   *Rocky Roads: The Journeys of Families through Suicide Grief* (Chellehead Works, 2010)

>   *A Winding Road: A Handbook for Those Supporting the Suicide Bereaved,* co-authored with John Peters, M. Suicidology (Chellehead Works, 2010)

>   *Seeking Hope: Stories of the Suicide Bereaved,* co-edited with Julie Cerel, PhD (Chellehead Works, 2010). Proceeds of this book benefit a fund at the American Association of Suicidology for suicide bereavement research.

The Samaritans, www.samaritanusa.org

>   Samaritans Centers "provide volunteer-staffed hotlines, professional and volunteer-run public education programs, 'suicide survivor' support groups and many other crisis response, outreach and advocacy activities and programs to the communities we serve."[1]

Coping with Difficult Times

Tara Brach, *Finding True Refuge: Meditations for Difficult Times,* Audio CD (2013) (www.SoundsTrue.com)

Pema Chodron, *When Things Fall Apart: Heart Advice for Difficult Times* (Shambhala, reprint ed., 2000)

---

[1] All quotes in this chapter are from the resource's website unless otherwise noted.

Julia Cook, *The Ant Hill Disaster* (kids' book) (National Center for Youth Issues, 2014)

Clarissa Pinkola Estés, PhD, *The Faithful Gardener: A Wise Tale about That Which Can Never Die* (HarperOne, 2005)

Anne Lamott, *Stitches: A Handbook on Meaning, Hope and Repair* (Riverhead, 2013)

Elizabeth Lesser, *Broken Open: How Difficult Times Can Help Us* Grow (Villard, reprint ed. 2005)

Steven M. Taylor, *Out of the Darkness: From Turmoil to Transformation* (Hay House, 2011)

Coping with Grief

Julia Cook, *Grief is Like a Snowflake* (kids' book) (National Center for Youth Issues, 2011)

Diana deRegnier, *Mortimer Loses a Friend* (kids' book) (CreateSpace Independent Publishing Platform, 2013)

Joan Didion, *The Year of Magical Thinking* (Vintage, 2007)

Kathryn A. Markell and Marc A. Markell, *The Children Who Lived: Using Harry Potter and Other Fictional Characters to Help Grieving Children and Adolescents* (Routledge, 2008)

Audrey Stringer, www.astringofhope.com

Get Over It! Surviving Grief to Live Again (A String of Hope, Inc., 2005)

Scaling the Mountain of Grief: Creating a New Normal through Loss and Healing (A String of Hope, Inc., 2012)

Kevin Young, editor, *The Art of Losing: Poems of Grief and Healing* (Bloomsbury USA, 2010)

The Compassionate Friends, www.compassionate friends.org

"When a child dies, at any age, the family suffers intense pain and may feel hopeless and isolated. The Compassionate Friends provides highly personal comfort, hope, and support to every family experiencing the death of a son or a daughter, a brother or a sister, or a grandchild, and helps others better assist the grieving family." Local chapters worldwide, online support and resources, annual conferences.

Helping Parents Heal, www.helpingparentsheal.info

Helping Parents Heal is a non-profit organization dedicated to assisting parents who have lost children, giving them support and resources to aid in the healing process. They "go a step beyond other groups by allowing the open discussion of spiritual experiences and evidence for the afterlife, in a non-dogmatic way." Local chapters, online support, and resources offered.

The Prayer Registry, www.sheriperl.com/the-prayer-registry (for parents who have lost a child)

Death and Dying

Betty J. Kovacs, PhD, *The Miracle of Death* (Kamlak Center, 2003)

Elisabeth Kübler-Ross, MD, *Death: The Final Stage of Growth* (Scribner 1997)

Stephen and Ondrea Levine, http://levinetalks.com

Multiple books and meditation CDs on the topics of death, dying, forgiveness, and compassion

Finding Happiness

Shawn Achor, *Before Happiness: The 5 Hidden Keys to Achieving Success, Spreading Happiness, and Sustaining Positive Change* (Crown Business, 2013)

Tal Ben-Shahar, PhD, *Being Happy: You Don't Have to Be Perfect to Lead A Rich, Happier Life* (McGraw-Hill, 2010)

Peter Fairfield, *Deep Happy: How to Get There and Always Find Your Way Back* (Weiser Books, 2012)

Gretchen Rubin, *The Happiness Project: Or, Why I Spent a Year Trying to Sing in the Morning, Clean My Closets, Fight Right, Read Aristotle, and Generally Have More Fun* (Harper Paperbacks, 2011)

Martin E. P. Seligman, PhD, *Authentic Happiness: Using the New Positive Psychology to Realize Your Potential for Lasting Fulfillment* (Atria Books, 2004)

Peter Spinogatti, *Explaining Unhappiness: Dissolving the Paradox* (iUniverse, 2010)

Funeral Etiquette

Kay Lewis, *Funeral Etiquette . . . The Quick and Easy Reference Guide* (CreateSpace Publishing Platform, 2013)

Mental Health

Fountain House, www.fountainhouse.org

> NYC community-based organization, "Dedicated to the recovery of men and women with mental illness by providing opportunities for our members to live, work, and learn while contributing their talents through a community of mutual support."

NAMI, www.nami.org

> The National Alliance on Mental Illness is the "nation's largest nonprofit, grassroots mental health education, advocacy, and support organization dedicated to mental illness." Support, discussion groups, resources, veteran help, and more.

Postpartum Depression and Maternal Well-Being

Yael Daphna Saar's online support forum: www.mamascomfortcamp.com

The Seleni Institute, http://seleni.org

> Mental health and wellness support for women and their families; online emotional support, advice, and information; and research funding. Counseling, workshops, and lectures provided in the Greater New York City area.

Katherine Stone's blog: www.postpartumprogress.com

Self-Help

Tara Brach, *Radical Acceptance: Embracing Your Life with the Heart of Buddha* (Bantam, 2004)

Brené Brown, PhD, LMSW

> *Daring Greatly: How the Courage to be Vulnerable Transforms the Way We Live, Love, Parent, and Lead* (Gotham, 2012)

> *The Gifts of Imperfection: Let Go of Who You Think You're Supposed to Be and Embrace Who You Are* (Hazelden, 2010)

> *I Thought It Was Just Me (But It Isn't): Making the Journey from "What Will People Think?" to "I Am Enough"* (Gotham, 2007)

Julia Cook, www.JuliaCookonline.com

> Kids' books on life issues, overcoming fears, personal behaviors, health and mental health issues, dealing with parents, technology issues, and activity books, including:
>
> *Blueloon* (kids' book on depression) (National Center for Youth Issues, 2012)
>
> *Wilma Jean the Worry Machine* (kids' book on anxiety) (National Center for Youth Issues, 2012)

James S. Gordon, MD, *Unstuck: Your Guide to the Seven-Stage Journey Out of Depression* (Penguin, 2009)

Sandra Ingerman, *How to Heal Toxic Thoughts: Simple Tools for Personal Transformation* (Sterling Publishing, 2007)

Robert Augustus Masters, PhD, *Emotional Intimacy: A Comprehensive Guide for Connecting with the Power of Your Emotions* (Sounds True, 2013)

Caroline Myss

> *Anatomy of the Spirit: Seven Stages of Power and Healing* (Harmony, 1997)
>
> *Why People Don't Heal and How They Can* (Harmony, 1998)

Don Miguel Ruiz, *The Four Agreements: A Practical Guide to Personal Freedom* (Amber-Allen Publishing, 1997)

Ronald D. Siegel, PsyD, *The Mindfulness Solution: Everyday Practices for Everyday Problems* (Guilford, 2009)

Colin Tipping *Radical Forgiveness: A Revolutionary Five-Stage Process* (rev. ed., Sounds True, 2010)

> www.RadicalForgiveness.com—worksheets, trainings, and assorted resources

Eckhart Tolle, *The Power of Now:* A Guide to Spiritual Enlightenment (New World Library, 2004)

Celeste Yacoboni, editor, *How Do You Pray? Inspiring Responses from Religious Leaders, Spiritual Guides, Healers, Activists and Other Lovers of Humanity* (Monkfish Book Publishing, 2014)

www.HealthJourneys.com

> Wide array of guided imagery CDs for health and well-being, many of which are used in hospitals across the country and have been tested for their efficacy.

www.HeartMath.org

> "Dedicated to improving health, performance, and well-being at home and in

the workplace. We provide products and services that enable people to transform stress, better regulate emotional responses and harness the power of heart/brain communication. Through our training programs, coaching, publications, licensing programs and innovative technology we provide practical, scientifically validated methods that enable people to live more rewarding, healthy and productive lives personally and professionally."

Sexual Abuse

Carolyn Lehman, *Strong at the Heart: How It Feels to Heal from Sexual Abuse* (Farrar, Straus and Giroux, 2005)

Nancy J. Napier, *Getting Through the Day: Strategies for Adults Hurt as Children* (W. W. Norton, 1994)

Spiritual Abuse

Boyd Purcell, PhD, *Spiritual Terrorism: Spiritual Abuse from the Womb to the Tomb* (AuthorHouse, 2008)

Trauma

Judith Herman, *Trauma and Recovery: The Aftermath of Violence—from Domestic Abuse to Political Terror* (Basic Books, 1997)

Peter A. Levine and Ann Frederick, *Waking the Tiger: Healing Trauma* (North Atlantic Books, 1997)

Aphrodite T. Matsakis, PhD, *I Can't Get Over It: A Handbook for Trauma Survivors* (New Harbinger Publications, 1996)

Belleruth Naparstek, *Invisible Heroes: Survivors of Trauma and How They Heal* (Bantam, 2005)

Robert Scaer, *The Body Bears the Burden: Trauma, Dissociation, and Disease* (Routledge, 3rd ed., 2014)

Bessel van der Kolk, MD, *The Body Keeps Score: Brain, Mind, and Body in the Healing of Trauma* (Viking Adult, 2014)

Elizabeth G. Vermiliyea, *Growing Beyond Survival: A Self-Help Toolkit for Managing Traumatic Stress* (Sidran Press, 2000)

International Society for the Study of Trauma and Dissociation (ISSTD), www.isst-d.org

Veterans and Their Families

Sgt. Stephanie J. Shannon, *Battling the Storm Within* (Stepeze Enterprise, 2014)

Joseph Bobrow, www.cominghomeproject.net

Edward Tick, PhD

War and the Soul: Healing Our Nation's Veterans from Post-traumatic Stress Disorder (Quest Books, 2005)

Warrior's Return: Restoring the Soul from War (Sounds True, 2014)

Soldiers Heart offers retreats, support, community-based services, veteran-to-veteran mentoring, healing journeys to Viet Nam, training, lectures, and more. www.soldiersheart.net

Belleruth Naparstek, *Healing Trauma: Guided Imagery for PTSD,* Audio CD (Health Journeys, 1999)

www.healthjourneys.com. Discounts for military and their families.

Tragedy Assistance Program for Survivors: Caring for the families of our fallen heroes (TAPS), www.taps.org

"TAPS provides immediate and long-term emotional help, hope, and healing to all who are grieving the death of a loved one in military service to America. TAPS meets its mission by providing peer-based emotional support, grief and trauma resources, casework assistance, and connections to community-based care." Online community support, 24/7 support 800-959-8277, grief camp, mentoring, and more.

Widows

Carole Brody Fleet, www.widowswearstilettos.com

Co-authored with Syd Harriet, PhD, PsyD, *Widows Wear Stilettos: A Practical and Emotional Guide for the Young Widow* (New Horizon Press, 2009)

Co-authored with Lisa Kline, *Happily EVEN After: A Guide to Getting Through (and Beyond) the Grief of Widowhood* (Viva Editions, 2012)

Working on the Soul Level

Afterlife

Eben Alexander, MD, *Proof of Heaven: A Neurosurgeon's Journey into the Afterlife* (Simon & Schuster, 2012)

Sally Baldwin, *Dying to Live Again* (Green Parrot Press, 2001)

Roland M. Comtois, *And Then There Was Heaven: A Journey of Hope and Love* (Chalice Communications, 2009)

Helen Greaves, *Testimony of Light: An Extraordinary Message of Life after Death* (Tarcher, 2009)

Anita Moorjani, *Dying to Be Me: My Journey from Cancer, to Near Death, to True Healing* (Hay House, 2012)

Ron Pappalardo, *Reconciled by the Light: The After-Death Letters from a Teen Suicide* (2009)

Sheri Perl, *Lost and Found: A Mother Connects-Up with Her Son in Spirit* (Perl Publications, 2011)

Past lives

Bruce Leininger, Andrea Leininger, and Ken Gross, *Soul Survivor: The Reincarnation of a World War II Fighter Pilot* (Grand Central Publishing, 2010)

Brian L. Weiss, MD

Many Lives, Many Masters: The True Story of a Prominent Psychiatrist, His Young Patient, and the Past-Life Therapy That Changed Both Their Lives (Fireside, 1988)

Miracles Happen: The Transformational Healing Power of Past Life Memories (HarperOne, 2012)

Roger Woolger, PhD

Healing Your Past Lives: Exploring the Many Lives of the Soul (Sounds True, 2010)

Other Lives, Other Selves: A Jungian Psychotherapist Discovers Past Lives (Bantam, 1988)

Individual Practitioners

This is a small list of individuals who work on the soul level in a variety of ways. They each offer an assortment of gifts, talents, and services, ranging from soul readings, mediumship, channeling, intuitive work, and healing, to past lives with karmic implications, and soul work. Please visit their websites for a better understanding of their respective offerings:

John Bannon, www.cpt.uk.com

Natalie K. Gianelli, http://nataliegianelli.com

Marcia A. Manoogian, www.marciaamanoogian.com

Christine Page, MD, www.christinepage.com

Joan Pancoe, http://joanpancoe.com

Carol Ritberger, PhD, www.ritberger.com

Jade Wah'oo Grigori, jadewahoo@shamanic.net

Linda A. Warren, www.lindaawarren.com

Patricia Windom, www.patwindom.com

Acknowledgments

One of the individuals whose story is included in the book asked me why it has taken me so long to write this book (almost three years), as he had completed six books in the time it has taken me to do one. I had to smile. This book has, indeed, been a journey for me.

Initially, talking about suicide was like crawling on my belly over barbed wire and broken glass. It was painful and sad. It hurt in every way. But something happened through all the conversations: redemption, possibility, and, ironically and counterintuitively, a call to life came to the surface. How do we interact and interface with one another following a suicide, any sudden death, heartbreak, or tragedy? What is our relationship with life? How do we create anew? The exploration of suicide has opened my eyes and stretched my heart in more ways than I can name.

Writing this book has been a practice of deepening as well as opening for me. So many people have helped me. Thank you, all of you, for the myriad of ways that you have aided, abetted, and supported this process. I am most grateful.

You have pointed me in the right direction. You have suggested a book, a person, a film, a song, a resource, and a point of view. You have provided me with a space to write and have been a lovely distraction (I am especially talking to you, Bonny and Hamish).

You have been a bridge, another perspective, a counterpoint, a voice of encouragement, and an expert. You have come from around the world and have talked to me from the bottom of your heart and the depths of your soul. You have shared your story, your path, your experience, and your wisdom. You are the grace notes of this book.

I am incredibly blessed, deeply humbled, and mightily thankful to all of you wonderfully generous and open-hearted people. Many of you even wore multiple "help desk" hats. Thank you for all of your help. Thank you. Thank you.

In particular, thank you to: Louise DeLoache Actkinson, Alyssa Baccarini, Laura Wooster Baldwin, Sally Baldwin, John Bannon, Melissa Bell, Grace Benz, Christine Biddle, Deborah Chamberlain, Roland Comtois, Mary Conlon, Debbie Cook, Julia Cook, Bill Corbett, Renee Corley, Paul Cronin, David Cumes, Anjela J. Dale, Carl David, Mona Delfino, Kathleen DiGiovanna, Jeaninne Englehart, Lynne Elwinger, Peter Fairfield, Marcie Fallek, Judy Finneran, Carole Brody Fleet, Natalie K. Gianelli, Ivan M. Granger, Cathryn Green, Elizabeth Gricus, Jennifer Hancock, Scott Harrison, Louise Heidenreich, Connie Hernandez, Rania James, Terri Jay, Anthoula Katsimatides, Norine Krasnogor, Karen Larkin Johnson, Kay Lewis, Nitzia S. Logothetis, Stefania Massoni, Mary McManus, Kelly Meister, Walter G. Meyer, Pat Mitchell, Jacqueline Mosher, Antonia Nelson, Larry Nelson, Joyce O'Neill, Margareth Ornitz, Christine Page, Joan Pancoe, Yvonne Pepin-Wakefield, Anne Rita Pickard, Barry Popkin, Boyd Purcell, Mohanalakshmi Rajakumar, Starr Rexdale, Anne Preciado Rich, Carol Ritberger, Shirley Robinson, Betty Rothberg, Risa Ruse, Yael Daphna Saar, Lynn Sands, Fran Weems Sawdei, Beryl Shaw, Stephanie Shannon, Rhonda Smith, Beverly Searcy Spillyards, Peter Spinogatti, Loretta Stagen, Audrey Stringer, Marguerite Theophil and the W-E-A-V-E women, Edward Tick, Dianna Vagianos Armentrout, Sheri VanMeveren, Nicky VanValkenburgh, Audrey Vitolins, Lila Walker, Maillie Waters, Pat Windom, S. Woolley, Na'ama Yehuda, and Jacob Young.

And special huzzahs and shout-outs to

My team from the Other Side:

Jane, for the wave of affirmation

E, for your beneficence on all levels

My book team:

Meredith Blevins, Wild West cowgirl and mother hen, who created a fabulous cover and added her deft hand and sense of flow to the editing process

Carol Leyba, my personal Oz, who brought it all home and made it wonderfully tangible as lay-out designer, final-read editor, and printing mentor

Marie Moulton, aka "Liquid Sunshine," my longstanding professional right hand, for her steadfast support, ease, and good humor in juggling details, techie tangles, and all things needed to help get the word out into the world

Heidi Schulman, longtime friend, writer, and mother of the pink-tutu'd Tillie Marie, for her excellent resources and reminders about timing and process

My inspiration team:

My clients, who bring out my best self and forever teach me the real deal in countless ways

Colleen Brown, for being a guiding hand and a font of wisdom and encouragement from day one

Diana deRegnier, for opening the door even wider by sharing her truth and introducing me to The Compassionate Friends organization

Caroline Myss and Linda Paladin, for introducing me to the life of David Chethlahe Paladin and sharing his "Call back your spirit or die" story, the best healing story on the planet

Linda Warren, for being my insightful and fun cosmic soul sister in the dance

Gayook Liu Wong, for being my wise and honoring walk-along confidante throughout the birthing process of this book

My support team

Always and forever, my sister, Anne, my best gift ever, and my brother-in-law, Kevin, for making so much possible

My friends, near and far, for being there, noisy and loving, and making life so much fun and so very worthwhile

Now, would you all stand, please? Take a bow. You more than deserve it. Can you feel the love? I certainly hope so. I couldn't have done it without you. Humbled, awed, and thrilled for this many-year endeavor to reach completion and this book to come to life. Thank you for making it possible. Each and every one of you holds a special place in my heart.

Adele's take-aways

1. Ask for a helping hand when needed.

2. Honor and allow.

3. Nothing is unbearable if it can be shared.

4. Remember, you have to feel to heal.

5. Speak from the heart.

6. Stay safe.

7. Stay sane.

8. Trust your good instincts and intuition.

About the author

ADELE RYAN McDOWELL, PhD, is a psycho-therapist with 30+ years of experience. Adele was the director of outpatient treatment at Liberation Clinic, a substance abuse clinic in Stamford, Connecticut. She was also the founder/director of The Greenheart Center, a holistic, psychotherapeutic, and psycho-educational center in Stamford.

Dr. McDowell's work focuses on helping clients find hope, balance, and peace in the face of crisis, trauma, abuse, and grief. She has worked with suicide, domestic violence, and sexual assault crisis hotlines; survivors of Hurricane Katrina, 9/11, the Joplin Tornado, and the Newtown shooting; clients struggling with addiction and heartbreak, as well as those moving through profound life changes such as grief and health challenges.

Dr. McDowell is the author of *Balancing Act: Reflections, Meditations, and Coping Strategies for Today's Fast-Paced Whirl*. The suicide of a fellow psychologist led to the creation of her second book, *Making Peace with Suicide: A Book of Hope, Understanding, and Comfort*.

Adele lives in Connecticut where she maintains a private practice.

You can learn more about Adele, her writing, and her thinking at http://AdeleRyanMcDowell.com and http://AdeleandthePenguin.com. You may contact Adele at P.O. Box 385, Riverside, CT 06878.

More by Adele Ryan McDowell

BALANCING ACT:

Reflections, Meditations, and Coping Strategies for Today's Fast-Paced Whirl

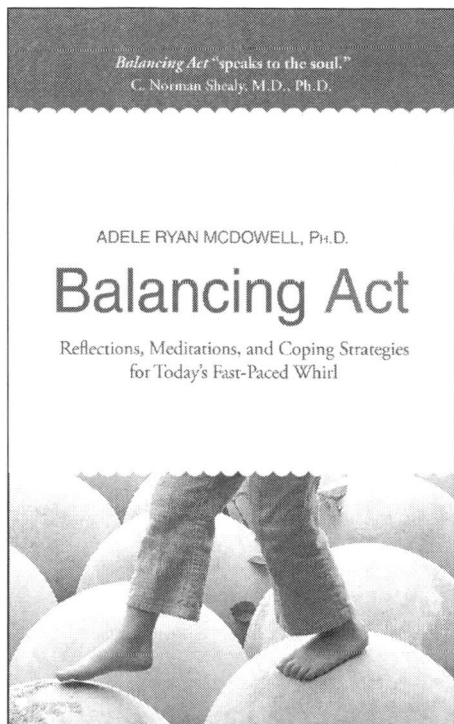

Balancing Act is an indispensable resource for handling stress and strain. It is practical, comforting, and humorous mind-body wisdom—a must-have for your bedside table.

C. Norman Shealy, MD, PhD, says *Balancing Act* "speaks to the soul."

Bernie Siegel, MD:
". . . can help to inform you and inspire change."

Dr. Frank Lawlis:
". . . is well worth reading. . . ."

Carol Ritberger, PhD
". . . is one book you will read multiple times."

In *Balancing Act*, you will find reflections, meditations, and coping strategies grounded in psychoneuroimmunology, cognitive-behavioral, transpersonal, and positive psychologies, big-picture spirituality, and humor to help you make it through the day—as well as the night.

Published by White Flowers Press (2011).
ISBN: 1452532168, 9781452532165.

Available from Amazon, Barnes & Noble, Books-A-Million, IndieBound, and independent bookstores.

See also http://makingpeacewithsuicide.com